Endorsements of
Bead by Bead: The Scriptural Rosary

"*Bead by Bead* is an excellent resource for helping us all better appreciate and pray the Mysteries of the Rosary."

FR. MICHAEL GAITLEY, MIC
Author of *33 Days to Morning Glory*

"In this centenary anniversary of the appearance of the Blessed Virgin Mother at Fatima, Meggie K. Daly has given to the Church and the world a beautiful gift in the form of her book, *Bead by Bead: The Scriptural Rosary.* Increasingly, numerous Catholics have discovered the Holy Scriptures as an encounter with Christ— Meggie has delivered a book which unites the twin gifts of the Word of God and the Holy Rosary—a beautiful and powerful combination leading to holiness. In our turn, we can respond to Our Lady of the Rosary by praying the Scriptural Rosary, fulfilling our Lady's request at Fatima by bringing to life the teaching of St. John Paul II, 'The Rosary is a Gospel prayer.'"

JOHN GALTEN
National President of Militia Immaculata, USA

"Meggie K. Daly's *Bead by Bead: The Scriptural Rosary* is more than just a devotional aid; it provides a brief history of the Rosary in addition to her testimony from rosary skeptic to devotee. She shares the fruit of her experience with the Rosary after discovering the richness of the saints and their devotion to Mary. Meggie K. Daly leads the reader into an experience of the Rosary as a prayer experience rooted in the Scriptures. The pages of the Gospel will certainly come alive for anyone who reads and uses this book."

FR. EDWARD LOONEY
Author of the best-selling rosary devotional *A Rosary Litany*

"Meggie K. Daly's *Bead by Bead: The Scriptural Rosary* is a terrific resource for anyone who wants to take their daily recitation of the Rosary to a whole different—and higher—level. Using this book, the reader has at his/her disposal a line of Scripture for each bead that will help the reader to reflect more deeply on the mysteries and prayers of the Holy Rosary. Includes background, history, resources and an appendix, as well as the author's journey towards a Scriptural Rosary. Highly recommend!"

ELLEN GABLE HRKACH
Author, editor, publisher, past president of the
Catholic Writers Guild

Bead by Bead:
The Scriptural Rosary

Meggie K. Daly

Misericordia Publishing
Nashville, Tennessee

Cover design: James Hrkach

Cover art: The Virgin and Child, by Bernard van Orley (circa 1491/1492-1542), Museo del Prado-Ointura, Madrid, Spain, Art Resource N.Y.

All images are used with permission.

ISBN: 978-0-692-84525-7 (Full Color Print Edition)
ISBN: 978-0-692-89017-2 (Black & White Print Edition)
ISBN: 978-0-692-84526-4 (Digital Edition)

To all my mothers:

Mary, *my spiritual mother,*
who leads me to Jesus through her Immaculate Heart.
Ann, *my biological mother,*
who chose life instead of abortion.
Helen, *my adoptive mother,*
who loved me as if I were the daughter of her own flesh.

May the souls of Ann and Helen rest in peace.

Cuappa, Nicaragua, April 1980

During the first apparition of Mary, Bernardo [Martinez] was informed by Mary that she wanted people to pray the rosary every day. She also informed him that she was not pleased when the rosary was prayed mechanically or in a rushed manner and recommended that Bernardo and others pray the rosary with the aid of biblical excerpts. Not knowing exactly what Mary meant, Bernardo confessed to Our Lady that he was unaware that the rosary was a biblical prayer ... [1]

~ Donald. H. Calloway, MIC
Champions of the Rosary

CONTENTS

In this book, the author capitalizes the word "rosary" when its usage refers to the devotion and is used as a noun. If the word "rosary" refers to the physical set of beads or is used an as adjective, then the author does not use capitalization.

No attempt has been made to standardize the capitalization of the word "rosary" in excerpts from other sources.

ACKNOWLEDGMENTS

Permission is gratefully acknowledged to cite from the copyrighted publications and digital media listed below. Without the generosity of these individuals and publishers, this book would not be possible.

Excerpts from *The World's First Love (2nd edition): Mary, Mother of God*, Venerable Fulton J. Sheen, (San Francisco, CA: Ignatius Press, 2011), are used with permission of Ignatius Press. The quote, found on page xiii, is taken from page 215 of *The World's First Love (2nd edition): Mary, Mother of God*.

Excerpts from *Champions of the Rosary*, Donald. H. Calloway, MIC, (Marian Press, Stockbridge, MA, 2016), are used with permission of the Marian Fathers of the Immaculate Conception of the B.V.M. The excerpt, found on page v, is taken from page 148 of *Champions of the Rosary*.

Excerpts from *The Secret of the Rosary*, St. Louis de Montfort, trans. Mary Barbour, T.O.P., (Charlotte, NC: St. Benedict Press, 1987), are used with permission of TAN Books.

Excerpts from *True Devotion to Mary: With Preparation for Total Consecration*, St. Louis de Montfort, trans. Fr. Frederick William Faber, D.D., (Charlotte, NC: St. Benedict Press, 2010), are used with permission of TAN Books.

Excerpt from *The Everlasting Man*, G.K. Chesterton, (Nashville, TN: Sam Torode Book Arts, 2014), is used with permission of Sam Torode Book Arts.

Excerpt from Lighthouse Talk, *Vatican II, Mercy, and You*, Fr. Michael Gaitley, MIC, (Greenwood Village, CO: Augustine Institute, 2016), is used with permission of Fr. Michael Gaitley, MIC, and the Augustine Institute.

Excerpt from *Lectio Prayer: Finding Intimacy with God*, Tim Gray, (Greenwood Village, CO: Augustine Institute, 2016), is used with permission of the Augustine Institute.

IN GRATITUDE

My serendipitous discovery of *The Scriptural Rosary for the Sorrowful Mysteries for Justice* on the United States Conference of Catholic Bishops website was a key inspiration for this book.[1] *The Scriptural Rosary for the Sorrowful Mysteries for Justice* pairs a biblical verse with each bead of the rosary, except for the *Glory Bes*, incorporating specific Scripture selected for its emphasis on social justice.

Due to Fr. Michael Gaitley's book, *33 Days to Morning Glory*, I consecrated myself to Jesus through the Immaculate Heart of Mary and eventually developed the discipline to begin praying the Rosary.[2] The entire video-based Hearts Afire Parish-based Retreat Program, which I facilitated in my home parish, was an incubator for my relentless search to understand why it is that Mary wants us to pray the Rosary.[3]

Fr. Donald Calloway's book, *Champions of the Rosary*, provided me with a trusted and thoroughly researched history of the Rosary and its prayers.[4] This book satisfied my growing desire to be connected with others who have loved the Rosary over the centuries, and it enabled me to write the short history of the Rosary contained in this book. For readers who wish to dig deeply into the history of the Rosary, I strongly recommend the book, *Champions of the Rosary*.

My love of Scripture matured along with my Christian faith. I am very grateful for those years, after my initial conversion experience, when I worshiped with my Protestant Christian brothers and sisters. Their passion for, and study of, God's written Word was incredibly contagious and a valuable model for me.

Leading biblical scholars such as Scott Hahn, Mary Healy, Tim Grey, Brandt Pitre, Edward Sri, and many others have further fueled my love for Sacred Scripture and brought me to a fuller understanding than I would have achieved on my own. Without these great teachers, I would have missed some of the important connections between the Old and the New Testament Scriptures.

I wish to thank those who read earlier copies of this manuscript to provide feedback and encouragement. At the top of the list is Ellen Gable Hrkach for her assistance in editing and for her cheerleading skills. Many thanks to Doug Garrett, John Galten,

Fr. Edward Looney, and Linda Watson for their supportive and helpful comments.

I am grateful to Sarah Chichester for making the impossible, possible, and to Fr. Michael Gaitley for taking the time to review my manuscript amidst the craziness of his schedule. Accolades go to James Hrkach, the cover artist, who transformed my rough vision into the final stunning cover.

Karina Fabian provided the final polishing edits to the manuscript which, to my amazement, even included reading it backward.

Thanks are due to my husband, who graciously overlooked my less-than-diligent approach to housekeeping during parts of this project, and who also provided help in proofreading.

Finally, I want to acknowledge that without the mercy of God and the intercession of all those who prayed for me to receive the gift of faith, my life would be governed by anxiety and driven by the desire for the approval of others; I would lack repentance for my sins and the benefit of the sacraments to help me on my journey to my final home. I shall forever be awestruck by the loving and merciful gaze of Christ. He is the greatest desire of my heart. For this, I am eternally grateful.

*No normal mind yet has been overcome by worries or fears who was faithful to the rosary. You will be surprised how you can climb out of your worries, **bead by bead**, up to the very throne of the Heart of love itself (emphasis added).*

~ Venerable Fulton J. Sheen

CHAPTER 1

INTRODUCTION

Because the rosary is both a mental and a vocal prayer, it is one where intellectual elephants may bathe, and the simple birds may also sip.[1]
~ Venerable Fulton J. Sheen

The primary purpose of this book is to share Scripture that I have found extremely helpful to keep my meditations focused when I pray the Rosary. I include a separate chapter for each of the Mysteries of the Rosary: Joyful, Sorrowful, Glorious, and Luminous. Every single bead in the rosary, including the introductory prayers (the *Apostles' Creed, Our Father,* three *Hail Marys,* and the *Glory Be*), has a scriptural verse associated with it.

For each decade of the Rosary, I have inserted inspirational artwork that further enhances my meditations. The artwork recalls a time past when artists derived their greatest inspiration from the story of Salvation History, and the works of their hands were magnificent cathedrals and the awesome artwork that adorned them.

I have added in prayers before and at the end of each decade from St. Louis-Marie Grignion de Montfort's *The Secret of the Rosary.*[2] De Montfort's prayers help me to internalize a plea for sanctification specific to the particular decade of the Rosary that I am praying. I created my versions of the prayers before and at the end of each decade for the Luminous Mysteries, in de Montfort style, since these mysteries were not formally added to the Rosary until 286 years after his death.

1

I pray my Rosary, most often alone in my prayer room to limit distractions, with this book opened up to the appropriate Mysteries chapter for the day. As I recite the basic prayers of the Rosary quietly, almost in a whisper, I silently read and meditate on the scriptural verses that I have paired with each prayer bead. This additional activity of meditating on Scripture, while I am reciting the basic prayers of the Rosary, has an incredible power to calm my restless mind and guide it to the appropriate reflection.

For those who currently pray a daily Rosary, the *Scriptural Rosary* may help you to meditate more deeply on the Mysteries. You may find that it adds a lively freshness to your meditation experience.

For those who struggle to stay awake when praying the Rosary or suddenly find themselves thinking about something other than their rosary meditations (like me), this book may provide the extra stimulation needed for improved focus.

For those who have never been motivated to pray the Rosary but have a desire to do so, perhaps the power of Scripture can make what may seem a spiritual chore easier. What was once a burden for me has been transformed into something sweet such that I now look forward to the 20-30 minutes of total peace when I pray my daily Rosary.

I created the four Mysteries of the Rosary chapters in this book first and for my personal use only. However, one summer afternoon on the way up to my prayer room, I halted in response to an internal, yet almost audible question, "Why not publish your scriptural meditations?" Oddly enough it did not seem like it was my idea. The idea of sharing my newly created meditation aids was instantly appealing—exhilarating yet simultaneously calming. Moreover, the prospect of writing this book seemed easier than finishing the novel that I had neglected for two years.

As this "suggestion" morphed into a real project, I discovered that publishing a book containing Scripture has many necessary restrictions to respect the biblical publisher's copyright properly. In my case, I needed to keep the total word count for the scriptural verses strictly less than a particular percentage of the book's internal word count. Initially, that is why the four chapters, "Soil," "Seeds," "Fertilizer," and "Harvest," were composed and are included in this book—to increase the non-Scripture word count.

However, as I started writing the extra chapters, I realized that my audience for this little book had greatly expanded—at least in theory. The book might now appeal to non-Catholics with an interest in why Catholics bother to pray the "repetitious" Rosary. The book could be of service to poorly-formed Catholics who know nothing of the Rosary. For example, the majority of the members of my family neither pray the Rosary, know how to pray the Rosary, nor care to know how to pray the Rosary.

I can imagine my husband, passing out this book to all those attending my funeral, noting that my final request was that those at my funeral pray at least one Rosary for me. He could then add, "Meggie asked me to tell you that this little book can serve as your tutorial; it documents her journey from avoidance of the Rosary to a love of the Rosary." I must say that I like the idea of giving a reading assignment and homework at my funeral!

Growing Your Rosary Devotion

I have named the next four chapters borrowing from an analogy painfully reminiscent of my initial efforts to grow roses in the region of the U.S. that I now call home. It is beautiful in the South, but a humid climate and poorly draining clay soil are not a rose garden's best "friend." As you read these chapters, visualize Mother Mary leading you into your personal sacred rosarium following a trail of rosary beads (or rose petals). While the walk may at first seem strenuous, it becomes very easy, "fragrant," and beautiful. I promise.

The Soil: Short History of the Rosary. For readers who have never read a history of how the prayers of the Rosary developed or how the rosary devotion itself came to be, I encourage you to carve out time to read this chapter. Once my devotion to the Rosary blossomed, I became quite interested in how the Rosary came to be. I discovered that the Rosary is a magnificent work-in-progress by Our Blessed Mother and is far from a stagnant prayer. The Rosary has evolved over the centuries, and I expect that it will continue to do so.

The Seeds: Format and Basic Prayers. This chapter is the tutorial part of the book as it teaches those unfamiliar with the Rosary the basic prayers and their order among the beads. Readers familiar with the Rosary may skip this chapter altogether. But as many in this generation have never prayed the Rosary, I have incorporated this information for completeness. Although I don't use the most common concluding prayer for the Rosary, I include it in this chapter.

The Fertilizer: Essential Nutrients. This chapter provides anecdotal examples of the uphill battle that devotion to the Rosary faces in today's culture, inside and outside the Catholic Church, based on my personal observations. I identify certain events in my life that functioned as the "fertilizer" to prepare the "soil" of my rosary devotion. God, the Master Gardener, habitually worked the smallest, seemingly insignificant events into a bigger plan than I could ever anticipate. But in hindsight, I can give Him all the glory that His works so deserve! If we have eyes to see, ears to hear, and a willing pair of hands, He can use each of us mightily.

The Harvest: My Journey. This chapter is my rosary testimony. It chronicles my struggles to run from the Rosary and final triumph to incorporate the Rosary into my daily life. If you need some prodding or think that praying the Rosary is not within your grasp, then this chapter is for you.

If you persist in your efforts to pray the Rosary, devoutly, your Mother Mary will mold you into a saint...*bead by bead.*

CHAPTER 2

THE SOIL:
SHORT HISTORY OF THE ROSARY

The rosary is a spiritual weapon, a heavenly sword, fashioned by the hands of a Divine Craftsman. All swords take time and skill to make, but this heavenly sword required the greatest of efforts—centuries—to produce.[1]

~Donald. H. Calloway, MIC

The Rosary and its many prayers took centuries to develop into their present form. This evolution paralleled significant events in the history of the Christian world, in particular, when apostasy and socio-political upheaval were rampant. Apostasy is the abandonment or renunciation of the Christian faith and is a hallmark of our times. The Rosary has never been a stagnant prayer, petition or devotion. There is no reason to expect that the Blessed Mother should halt the development of her Rosary until Christ's second coming. In my lifetime, I witnessed the incorporation of the Luminous Mysteries—but I am getting ahead of myself.

The *Our Father*, the most well-known prayer of the Rosary, is revered by all Christians. Christ taught the *Our Father* to His apostles when they asked Him how they should pray, as recorded in Matthew (6:9-13) and Luke (11:1-4).

Historians agree that the first precursor of Christians using prayer beads was the use of *Paternoster* "beads" to pray 150 *Our*

5

Fathers. (*Paternoster* is Latin for *Our Father.*) Although not a Rosary, the use of Paternoster beads made the transition to the Rosary straightforward. The choice of 150 was selected to match the number of psalms in the Old Testament and was considered to be a suitable substitution for the breviary[2] for those who could not read. As early as the fifth century, these "beads," which initially consisted of a rope containing 150 knots, were used to count *Paternosters.* By the 11th century, this was a popular devotion.

A century later the *Marian Psalter* is documented as being used in certain monastic communities. The same *Paternoster* "beads" could be used to pray the 150 *Hail Marys* (or *Ave Marias*) which comprised the *Marian Psalter.* At this time, the *Hail Mary* consisted of only the angelic salutation at the Annunciation, "Hail Mary, full of grace, the Lord is with thee" (Luke 1:28), followed by Elizabeth's greeting to Mary at the Visitation, "Blessed art thou among women and blessed is the fruit of thy womb Jesus" (Luke 1:42). The merging of these two Scripture passages into the *Ave Maria* occurred sometime around the sixth century.

Devotions consisting of 150 *Our Fathers* or 150 *Hail Marys* coexisted around the time of the birth of Dominic De Guzman (1170-1221) in Spain. St. Dominic, as he is known, started the Dominican order or Order of the Preachers. Perhaps less well-known is that St. Dominic is credited with the origin of the Rosary as he was the first to "preach" the *Marian Psalter.* This approach to the *Marian Psalter* was entirely new and unique.

St. Dominic's "preaching" consisted of teaching about specific events in the life of Christ and the Virgin Mary while instructing his listeners to meditate on these same events while praying the *Marian Psalter.* Thus St. Dominic was the first person to introduce the meditative component to the decades. With the union of the meditations to the decades of *Hail Marys*, the Rosary was indeed born!

Dominican tradition and later the writings of Blessed Alan de La Roche (1428-1475), also a Dominican, tell of an encounter between Mary and St. Dominic whereby she handed him rosary beads and charged him with "preaching" her Psalter. She gave him the particular mysteries to "preach" about for the decades of the Rosary. These mysteries are the Joyful, Sorrowful, and Glorious Mysteries of the Rosary. The reported encounter between St. Dominic and Mary occurred at the end of three days of prayer and fasting by St. Dominic who was grieved over his failure to halt the Albigensian heresy infecting southern France during the 12th century.

19th century stained glass window/ Franz Mayer & Co./ Carlow Cathedral, Ireland / @Andreas F. Borchert creativecommons.org/ licenses/ by-sa/ 4.0-3.0-2.5-2.0-1.0.

By following Mary's instructions, St. Dominic began to experience great success in converting the Albigensians back to orthodoxy. The name "rosary" (rosarium or rose garden) was first used at this time. St. Dominic started a Confraternity of the Rosary to spread devotion to the Rosary. Over the centuries, the popularity of the Rosary would rise and fall as did various confraternities promoting devotion to the Rosary.

Before the onslaught of the Black Death in the 14th century, devotion to the Rosary had all but ceased. The tremendous social and spiritual upheaval that accompanied the decimation of 30% to 75% of Europe's population due to the bubonic plague, undoubtedly delivered a keen recognition of human mortality that fueled a resurgence in devotion to the Rosary. It was at this time that the latter part of the *Hail Mary* was developed, "Holy Mary Mother of God, pray for us sinners now and *at the hour of our death* (emphasis added)."

In addition to the devastation of the plague, the favorable outcome by Christians of several battles against Turkish forces, the most famous being the Battle of Lepanto in 1571, is credited with reviving interest in the Rosary. Since 1573 the Church has always recognized a feast associated with the "Holy Rosary," although the name and day of the feast have been changed.

The Protestant Reformation of the 16th century had a deleterious effect on the popularity of the Rosary. One reason is that, by this time, praying the Rosary could be associated with indulgences, and the sale of indulgences was the watershed event for Martin Luther's breaking away from the Catholic Church. Although the Catholic Church outlawed the sale of indulgences in 1571, many modern-day Catholics do not understand the Catholic Church's teaching on indulgences—which are still a part of the "Treasury of the Saints."[3]

By the 17th century, the Rosary was neglected by lay and clergy alike. It was not uncommon for Catholic priests to ridicule piety to the Rosary devotion. It was during this time that St. Louis de Montfort (1673-1716) wrote his now cherished books and essays on the Rosary. He buried his writings in a field to safeguard them during the anti-clerical and tumultuous French Revolution. The books lay hidden and undisturbed until discovered in the early 20th century. Interestingly, St. Louis de Montfort suggested that other events of Christ's life could be used for mediation, including four of the five now found in the Luminous Mysteries of the Rosary.

On February 11, 1858, Our Lady began appearing to Bernadette Soubirous in Lourdes, France. During their time together, Bernadette reported that she and Our Lady would pray the Rosary together. The many miracles at Lourdes testified to the Church-sanctioned authenticity of Bernadette's visions and bolstered devotion to the Rosary.

Pope Leo XIII, known as "The Rosary Pope," issued 12 encyclicals and five apostolic letters on the Rosary, while promoting Our Lady of Lourdes during his papacy (1878-1903).[4]

Devotion to the Rosary was further increased in 1917 when Our Lady appeared several times to three shepherd children in Fatima, Portugal. During these Church-sanctioned apparitions, Mary implored the children to pray the Rosary:

I am the Lady of the Rosary, I have come to warn the faithful to amend their lives and ask for pardon for their sins. They must not offend Our Lord anymore, for He is already too grievously offended by the sins of men. People must say the Rosary. Let them continue saying it every day.[5]

Our Lady also asked the children to add the *Fatima Prayer* or *O My Jesus Prayer* at the end of each decade:

> *When you say the Rosary, say after each mystery: "O my Jesus, forgive us our sins, save us from the fires of Hell, and lead all souls to Heaven, especially those in most need of Thy mercy."* [6]

Ilustração Portuguesa, 29 October 1917. People looking at the Sun during the Fátima apparitions attributed to the Virgin Mary, Wikimedia Commons.

After Vatican II (1962-1965), the Rosary and all Marian devotions were viewed by many as obsolete and without value. Ironically Pope Paul VI (1963-78), who presided over the majority of Vatican II, issued the 1974 Apostolic Exhortation on Marian Devotion, *For the Right Ordering and Development of Devotion to the Blessed Virgin Mary (Marialis Cultus)*, which strongly encouraged praying the Rosary accompanied by prayerful meditation.[7]

The second successor of Paul VI, St. John Paul II (1978-2005) had a profound Marian devotion and issued an encyclical in 1987 on the *Mother of the Redeemer (Redemptoris Mater)*, which focused on Mary's role in the Church. In 2002, he issued the apostolic letter on the *Rosary of the Virgin Mary (Rosarium Virginis Mariae)*:

> *The Rosary, though clearly Marian in character, is at heart a Christocentric prayer. In the sobriety of its elements, it has all the depth of the Gospel message in its entirety, of which it can be said to be a compendium.*

> *It is an echo of the prayer of Mary, her perennial Magnificat for the work of the redemptive Incarnation which began in her virginal womb. With the Rosary, the Christian people ...[sit] at the school of Mary and ... [are] led to contemplate the beauty of the face of Christ and to experience the depths of his love. Through the Rosary the faithful receive abundant grace, as though from the very hands of the Mother of the Redeemer.[8]*

In St. John Paul II's apostolic letter of 2002, he also addressed the objections that arose after a misunderstanding of Vatican II's emphasis on the liturgy which caused many of the faithful to abandon the Rosary. St. John Paul II writes of a crisis in piety towards the Rosary, as well as a misunderstanding of Marian devotion:

> *The timeliness of this proposal is evident from a number of considerations. First, the urgent need to counter a certain crisis of the Rosary, which in the present historical and theological context can risk being wrongly devalued, and therefore no longer taught to the younger generation. There are some who think that the centrality of the Liturgy, rightly stressed by the Second Vatican Ecumenical Council, necessarily entails giving lesser importance to the Rosary. Yet, as Pope Paul VI made clear, not only does this prayer not conflict with the Liturgy, it sustains it, since it serves*

as an excellent introduction and a faithful echo of the Liturgy, enabling people to participate fully and interiorly in it and to reap its fruits in their daily lives.

Perhaps too, there are some who fear that the Rosary is somehow unecumenical because of its distinctly Marian character. Yet the Rosary clearly belongs to the kind of veneration of the Mother of God described by the Council: a devotion directed to the Christological centre [sic] of the Christian faith, in such a way that "when the Mother is honoured, the Son ... is duly known, loved and glorified." If properly revitalized, the Rosary is an aid and certainly not a hindrance to ecumenism![9]

In this same apostolic letter, *Rosarium Virginis Mariae*, the Luminous mysteries were introduced to help the faithful confront the time of great darkness of the world in the third millennium. Note that these very same mysteries were recommended by St. George Preca (1880-1962) before the Second Vatican Council. (St. Louis De Monfort made similar suggestions as noted previously.)

Although the Luminous Mysteries remain optional, I love praying the Rosary while meditating on the events from the ministry of Christ and admit that I often wondered at their absence.

There are two other very ancient Christian prayers included in our present-day Rosary: the *Apostles' Creed* (*Symbolum Apostolicum*) and the *Glory Be* (*Gloria Patri*). By the fourth century, both prayers acquired their current form with the exception of the phrase "maker of heaven and earth," which was added to the *Apostles' Creed* in the seventh century.

Letters from the third century demonstrate the existence of both prayers in the Christian communities. The *Glory Be* prayer has been documented as part of baptismal ceremonies as early as the second century. Illustrated manuscripts from the 13th century verify that a popular tradition held that each of the 12 Apostles wrote a part of the *Apostles' Creed* during or after Pentecost. Some historians have suggested that this tradition is rooted in the twelve statements of faith in the *Apostles' Creed*.

I can find no source to indicate exactly when the *Glory Be* and the *Apostles' Creed* were added into the Rosary. They do not appear to be part of the first rosary prayers but seem to be added in later. In the *Secret of the Rosary* written in the late 1700s, St. Louis de

Montfort makes mention of both the *Apostles' Creed* and the *Glory Be*.[10] At the time de Montfort wrote *The Secret of the Rosary*, the Rosary was taken to mean all 15 decades of the collective Joyful, Sorrowful, and Glorious Mysteries.

In the religious art from the 15th century, one often sees a very long strand of rosary beads with no crucifix or short part of the rosary that we associate with the opening prayers preceding the first decade. Other art from that period shows the addition of a crucifix but not the short part representing the opening prayers. Yet most sources say the format of the Rosary has been unchanged for five centuries up until the *Fatima Prayer* and then the Luminous Mysteries of the Rosary were added. That would seem to indicate that the opening prayers were part of the Rosary from the beginning.

The Rosary is a living prayer that has evolved over centuries and will continue to do so, if it pleases God, under the guidance of the Holy Spirit and Our Mother Mary, the spouse of the Holy Spirit. For a detailed discussion on the history of the Rosary, please see many of the excellent resources contained in the Appendix.

CHAPTER 3

THE SEEDS:
FORMAT AND BASIC PRAYERS

It is not just a conglomeration of Our Fathers and Hail Marys, but on the contrary it is a divine summary of the mysteries of the life, Passion, death, and glory of Jesus and Mary.[1]

~ St. Louis Mary de Montfort

Many readers may already be familiar with the mechanics of praying the Rosary. However, there may be others who do not know the basic prayers or how those prayers are combined into a Rosary. Although this chapter is a tutorial on the fundamentals, it is important to note that the Rosary has two important parts: recitation of the prayers (whether aloud or silently) and meditation on the Mysteries of the Rosary.

Without the meditations, the Rosary can become just a jumble of words. Granted, there are times when illness, intense physical pain, or insomnia leave us with little mental facility to do much more than walk one's fingers along rosary beads while mechanically reciting the prayers. Having developed the habit of praying the Rosary is a great blessing and comfort during such stressful times, and if we cannot meditate, then we can unite our suffering to His Cross whereby we identify our pain with His Passion.

This book focuses on those times when you do have the presence of mind to meditate. If you have the will, then this book may help you develop the skills to incorporate the Rosary into your daily life. By now you know enough of the history of the Rosary to understand the importance of both the prayers and the meditations, and, later I will share the technique that has helped me progress in my meditations on the Mysteries of the Rosary.

Praying the Rosary well means getting one's meditations on track in addition to saying the prescribed prayers.

Naturally, the more I can utilize all my senses when I pray the Rosary, the greater my attention and focus become. By fingering my rosary beads, I exploit my sense of touch while avoiding the distraction of counting individual prayers, thus keeping my mind free for meditations. When I say the prayers aloud, even if in a whisper, I use my voice and my hearing to help block out other distracting sounds. Rather than kneeling while praying the entire Rosary, I may substitute standing or sitting for alternate decades if in my prayer room. But if I am having a particularly good day, I find that I can pray the Rosary prayers in complete silence on my knees while focusing my meditations entirely on the Scriptures and sacred art.

The Mechanics of the Rosary

The prayers of the basic Rosary consists of the *Sign of the Cross*, one *Apostles' Creed*, six *Our Fathers*, 53 *Hail Marys*, and the six *Glory Be* prayers. The order of the prayers is important and are shown in the image on the next page.

Several other prayers have been added over time and are now considered to be part of the Rosary, although, in a strict sense, they are optional. The most popular of these include the *Fatima Prayer* and the *Hail, Holy Queen Prayer*. The *Fatima Prayer* is prayed at the end of each decade after the *Glory Be*.

The *Hail, Holy Queen* is prayed once at the end of the Rosary after the *Fatima Prayer* of the final decade. Introductory and concluding prayers are sometimes added; I have included some that are commonly used.

Each decade is announced prior to its start. For example, before the first *Our Father* for the first decade of the Sorrowful Mysteries, one says, "The first sorrowful mystery, The Agony in the Garden."

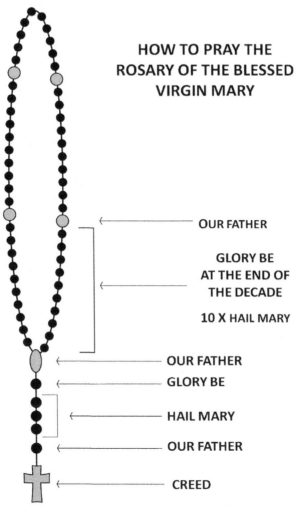

HOW TO PRAY THE ROSARY OF THE BLESSED VIRGIN MARY

← OUR FATHER

GLORY BE AT THE END OF THE DECADE

10 X HAIL MARY

← OUR FATHER

← GLORY BE

← HAIL MARY

← OUR FATHER

← CREED

© *Thoom / shutterstock.com*

Prayers of the Rosary

Sign of the Cross

In the name of the Father and of the Son and of the Holy Spirit, Amen. *(Use the crucifix of the rosary to touch the forehead, the lower chest, the left shoulder and then the right shoulder. At this point, I kiss the crucifix on my rosary, but some people kiss the crucifix before or after they make the Sign of the Cross.*)

Apostles' Creed

I believe in God, the Father Almighty, Creator of heaven and earth; and in Jesus Christ, his only Son, our Lord, who was conceived by the Holy Spirit, born of the Virgin Mary, suffered under Pontius Pilate, was crucified, died and was buried; he descended into hell; on the third day He rose again from the dead; he ascended into heaven, and is seated at the right hand of God the Father almighty; from there he will come to judge the living and the dead. I believe in the Holy Spirit, the Holy Catholic Church, the communion of saints, the forgiveness of sins, the resurrection of the body, and the life everlasting. Amen.

Our Father

Our Father, who art in heaven, hallowed be Thy name. Thy kingdom come: Thy will be done on earth as it is in heaven. Give us this day our daily bread. And forgive us our trespasses as we forgive those who trespass against us. And lead us not into temptation: but deliver us from evil. Amen.

Hail Mary (traditional form)

Hail Mary, full of grace, the Lord is with thee. Blessed art thou among women, and blessed is the fruit of thy womb, Jesus. Holy Mary, Mother of God, pray for us sinners, now and at the hour of our death. Amen.

Glory Be (Doxology)

Glory be to the Father, and to the Son, and to the Holy Spirit. As it was in the beginning, is now and ever shall be, world without end. Amen.

Fatima Prayer

O my Jesus, forgive us our sins, save us from the fires of hell, and lead all souls to Heaven, especially those in most need of Thy Mercy.

Hail, Holy Queen (Salve Regina)

Hail, holy Queen, Mother of mercy, our life, our sweetness and our hope. To thee do we cry, poor banished children of Eve. To thee do we send up our sighs, mourning and weeping in this valley of tears. Turn then, most gracious Advocate, thine eyes of mercy toward us, and after this our exile, show unto us the blessed fruit of thy womb, Jesus. O clement, O loving, O sweet Virgin Mary. Pray for us, O Holy Mother of God, that we may be made worthy of the promises of Christ. Amen.

Introductory or Concluding Prayer

O God, whose only begotten Son, by His life, death, and resurrection, has purchased for us the rewards of eternal life. Grant, we beseech Thee, that by meditating on these mysteries of the most holy Rosary of the Blessed Virgin Mary, we may imitate what they contain and obtain what they promise, through the same Christ our Lord. Amen.

Alternate Introductory Prayer According to the Method of St. Louis de Montfort

I unite myself with all the Saints in Heaven, and with all the just on earth; I unite myself with Thee, my Jesus, in order to praise Thy Holy Mother worthily and to praise Thee in her and by her. I renounce all the distractions that may come to me while I am saying this Rosary which I wish to say with modesty, attention, and devotion, just as if it were to be the last of my life. We offer Thee, O most Holy Trinity, this Creed in honor of all the mysteries of our faith, this Our Father and these three Hail Marys in honor of the unity of Thy Essence and the Trinity of Thy Persons. We ask of Thee a lively faith, a firm hope and an ardent charity. Amen.[2]

Alternate Concluding Prayer According to the Method of St. Louis de Montfort

We beseech Thee, dear Lord Jesus by the [...] mysteries of Thy life, passion and death, by Thy glory and by the merits of Thy Blessed Mother, to convert sinners and help the dying, to deliver the Holy Souls from Purgatory and to give us all Thy grace so that we may live well and die well—and please give us the Light of Thy Glory later on so that we may see Thee face to face and love Thee for all eternity. Amen. So be it.[3]

CHAPTER 4

THE FERTILIZER:
ESSENTIAL NUTRIENTS

For these men serve a mother who seems to grow more beautiful as new generations rise up and call her blessed.[1]

~G.K. Chesterton

Shortly after I moved from a large city on the West Coast of the United States to a small town in the Mid-Southern United States, I attended a Christmas party with my husband. Like many work-related holiday parties, we enjoyed the friendly thievery of a "Dirty Santa" gift exchange. Each of us was instructed to bring a gift of no more value than ten dollars to share if we wished to participate.

The only remarkable aspect of this gathering of merrymakers was that we were all part of an interdenominational pro-life Christian ministry. Since most in attendance were Baptists, the liquid cheer was absent, and duly noticed by the three Catholics present, of which by that time included my husband myself.

Towards the end of the gift exchange, a young woman selected the very smallest gift that had been passed over by everyone else. There was no ribbon to untie, and it was wrapped with newspaper instead of holiday wrapping like the other gifts. I thought to myself, "Bachelor-wrap, no doubt!" Its size and unimpressive presentation had secured its place among the last of the gifts to be chosen.

The gift surrendered its makeshift wrapping to reveal an old, but quite lovely, needlepoint zipper pouch in perfect condition. All eyes eagerly anticipated learning the contents of the pouch, as this was clearly not a gift purchased at Walmart like the others. With hurried fingers, she pulled out a gorgeous rosary.

She held the rosary up, not so much for everyone to see, but for her admiration, moved as she was by the beauty of the beads and intrigued by the crucifix. She had no idea of the purpose of the beads, but she instinctively knew they were something very special because of the crucifix. As she held up the rosary beads, she asked, "It is lovely. What is it?" Her eyes searched the small group for an answer.

A friend of my husband's, a middle-aged man and indeed a bachelor, quickly explained, "That's a rosary. It's a prayer old Catholic ladies say." He elaborated, "Each bead is a prayer. It belonged to my mother."

I felt a sense of sadness at his words. I knew this gentleman was very involved in Catholic religious education in his parish, and yet this was how he characterized the Rosary. Moreover, he had parted with what should have been a cherished family heirloom. I thought, "Well, I guess he doesn't pray the Rosary since old women do."

I pried my covetous gaze from the rosary to the giver and objected. "Lots of people pray the Rosary. It's not just a prayer for old ladies!" (I have yet to master the delicate tactfulness of a charming Southern-born woman.)

This interchange was not the best testimony to the little group of Baptist merrymakers who already had their reservations about Catholics. Our rosary-giver friend missed out on a great teaching opportunity at the Christmas party because Baptists love their Bible (and rightly so). Why? Because he had no idea that the Rosary is based on the Bible!

Now I fantasize that he might have said, "You have a mighty Christian sword in your hands there! It has the power to change the world. Catholics have been praying the Rosary for over 900 years, meditating on the greatest biblical mysteries of our Christian faith!" Possibly, such testimony may have even created a point for dialog later in a one-on-one setting. I suspect that, to him, the Rosary was just a monotonous repetition of the same few prayers.

At the time, I wasn't even praying the Rosary, and it had only been a couple of years since my return to the Catholic Church. However, his sentiments are shared by many men and women over the age of fifty who self-identify as Catholics whether they attend Mass or not. There are a variety of reasons that this is the case. It is not my intention to lay out every possible explanation for this disheartening trend, even if I knew them all, but rather, I hope to help reverse that trend in some small way.

Once I returned to the Catholic Church, my reluctance to pray the Rosary stemmed from my inability to meditate well on the mysteries. The Rosary has two parts that when united devoutly in our prayer, they render it a powerful weapon in the hands of our Mother Mary to combat evil in the world.

Yes, there is the recitation part of the Rosary, whether the prayers are vocalized aloud or silently, which is explained in the chapter, "The Seeds: Format and Basic Prayers". But there is also the essential meditative aspect, which I described in the chapter, "The Soil: Short History of the Rosary." Meditation is where I was deficient. It was not so much a lack of *will*, but a lack of *skill*. I do not think meditation just happens. We need to learn how to do it well.

Fr. Michael Gaitley, MIC, gave a talk during the Jubilee Year of Mercy declared by Pope Francis, that captures the potential of the Rosary:

> *And what is the Rosary but a prolonged meditation and prayer on the mysteries of the life of Christ revealed in the Gospels and that we are praying with she [Mary] who had the most enriched faith of all. [Praying the Rosary] is to contemplate the face of Christ in the mysteries of the Gospel with the eyes of Mary as an aid to helping us make the faith concrete and real. The Rosary is an amazing tool for the New Evangelization for the enrichment of faith because it is not just about studying the Word; it is praying the Word, meditating on the Word. It is contemplating Christ, so he comes into our hearts and into our lives so we can become other Christs which is the heart of New Evangelization.*[2]

Fr. Gaitley emphasizes three things: the meditative aspect of the Rosary, "seeing" the mysteries through the eyes of Mary, and the power of the Rosary to enrich our faith experience. He characterizes the Rosary as a "prolonged meditation" and an invitation to contemplate the "face of Christ." The companion Scriptures and images in this book have made it possible for me to visualize and ponder the Mysteries of the Rosary in a new way.

Meditation can produce a freedom from temporal constraints to join Mary and Jesus back in time, in at least as much as one becomes engrossed in a movie—and often much more so. I believe that the greater the quality of our meditations, the greater the gift the Rosary becomes for Mary, and the closer we come to Christ alongside Mary.

But if the Rosary is so powerful, why isn't it more popular?

I can only share three reasons that I have experienced directly or through interactions with others: spiritual laziness, improper grasp of the teachings of the Catholic Church on Mary, and lack of skill in meditation.

Spiritual Lethargy and the Catholic Hemorrhage

It takes discipline to acquire any good habit. Various studies report that it takes 21 days to two months to develop a new habit. I have found this to be the case when developing a spiritual discipline as well. Repetition is required to build up one's spiritual muscles. We need spiritual muscles for praying the Rosary. Allocating time to develop a spiritual discipline, like praying the Rosary well, is not easy in our frenzied culture. But beyond our hectic and digitally charged lifestyles, our spiritual vigor is not what it used to be as Catholics, as Christians, or even as "one nation under God." We have become a very secular society.

The block of people in the United States that self-identify as Catholics only weakly believe in the truths that distinguish Catholicism from Protestantism. Perhaps most shocking is the lack of belief by Catholics in the True Presence of Christ in the Eucharist. According to a 2008 survey by the Center for Applied Research in the Apostolate (CARA), at Georgetown University, Mass attendance is directly proportional to one's belief in the mysteries of our Catholic faith. I consider Mass attendance a measure of one's Catholic vigor and spiritual discipline, as well as trust in the mysteries of our Catholic faith.

Nine in ten weekly Mass attendees (91 percent) say they believe that Jesus Christ is really present in the Eucharist, compared to two-thirds of those who attend Mass less than weekly but at least once a month (65 percent), and four in ten of those attending Mass a few times a year or less (40 percent).[3]

Note the association between Mass attendance and belief in the Real Presence of Christ in the Eucharist. In general, increased Mass attendance is associated with a stronger belief in the Real Presence. If our Catholic community lacks faith in our greatest treasure, Christ's gift of Himself to us, then it is not surprising that devotion to the Rosary is weak as well.

For the first time in history, we are hemorrhaging more baptized Catholics than the acquisition of new Catholics through the RCIA process. Sherry Waddell makes that point in her book, *Forming Intentional Disciples*, and submits that our departing Catholics have headed into the ranks of Evangelical Christians.[4] That supposition resonated with my experience. I spent the first six years of my post-conversion "on-fire" Christian life in an Evangelical Church community where I met many other cradle Catholics such as myself.

A more recent study from the Pew Research Center reported the dismal statistic that between 2007 and 2014 there was a 3% drop in those who identify with the Catholic Church in any way. The raw numbers dropped from 54.3 to 50.9 million. And it is not just Catholics; self-identified Christians dropped from 78% to 71%.[5]

One of the most important factors in the declining share of Christians and the growth of the "nones" is generational replacement. As the Millennial generation enters adulthood, its members display much lower levels of religious affiliation, including less connection with Christian churches, than older generations. Fully 36% of young Millennials (those between the ages of 18 and 24) are religiously unaffiliated, as are 34% of older Millennials (ages 25-33). And fewer than six-in-ten Millennials identify with any branch of Christianity, compared with seven-in-ten or more among older generations, including Baby Boomers and Gen-Xers. Just 16% of Millennials are Catholic, and only 11% identify with mainline Protestantism. Roughly one-in-five are evangelical Protestants.[6]

For those who treasure their Catholic faith, rather than just ringing our hands in dismay, there is much we can do. We can start by learning and understanding our Catholic faith. There are a growing number of opportunities through programs like FORMED, created by the Augustine Institute, that allow a hungry Catholic to listen, read, watch, and enrich his faith anytime and any place with an Internet connection.[7]

Many cradle Catholics in my generation have a weak understanding of the Catholic faith. Ironically, plenty of those who have left the Catholic Church and entered the ranks of the "nones" believe that they truly understand the teachings of the Catholic Church. This includes some of my best friends and their significant others from my parochial school days when our high school religious education programs, such as CCD, were often devoid of any curriculum.

We must live our faith joyfully and be that attractive beacon of light to the dark world and to those who do not know the Lord. If we have given our children a poor example, we can humbly and sincerely apologize to them for own our mistakes/sins and start setting a good example.

If you want courage and wisdom, start praying the Rosary well. Moreover, you will enjoy the peaceful time that you spend in prayer. It is much easier to develop a habit that gives us pleasure!

Misunderstanding the Church's Teachings on Mary

Less than a year after the Christmas gift exchange incident (noted at the beginning of this chapter) and two days before the feast of the Assumption, I emailed out a meditation on the Assumption to a few of my Catholic friends. One recipient was a religious sister, some fifteen years my senior, who had taught for many years in a Catholic school near my childhood home at the time my children were in school. She quickly responded to my email, intent upon convincing me that the Assumption of Mary was not an infallible teaching of the Church and not all dioceses in the United Sates even celebrate the Assumption as a Holy Day of Obligation. I share that correspondence below:

This [Assumption of Mary] is a doctrine of faith but not infallible like the Immaculate Conception. The Pope has only used infallibility once and that is the Immaculate Conception doctrine. There is so much that is coming out from scientific and medical information that some things that a Catholic had to believe are now being questioned. I feel strongly that just like today there are unusual events and happenings. Many were just natural events which were overwhelming to a society that stayed mainly in place. The events of the heavens, water, etc. are still going on today but we think very little of it in relation to good or bad, punishing mankind, etc. I'm very cautious about taking things literally. In many places, it [Assumption] is no longer a holy day of obligation. America celebrates holy days much different from the rest of the world. This is one feast that isn't even a holy day in some parts of the United States.

The special days grew out of the immigrant needs to stay connected to their roots. The Mexicans today are bringing customs and special days which are being implemented by the priests which seem very foreign to many of us. The Mexicans are really into devotions while many of our churches have dropped devotionals and the young people were never taught some of the superstitious events around some of the saints. In fact today we emphasize people like Dorothy Day, Kateri Tekakwitha, Pope John the 23rd, Pope John Paul II, etc., and look more to the present day saints, such as Martin Luther King, Luther, etc. They challenged our thinking about the commandment to love God, our neighbor as well as ourselves. Thank you for sending me the article and I believe that Mary was honored and taken directly to heaven in some way and her example is there for us to emulate.

While Sister is a very kind and loving soul that has served the Church for many years unselfishly, she did not get the Assumption quite right. However, because she is a religious sister, many would take her as an expert witness on such matters. In 1950, Pope Pius XII made an infallible declaration regarding the Assumption of Mary in his Apostolic Constitution defining *ex cathedra* (from the chair of Peter), *Munificentissimus Deus*. Although this document is long, it is worth the read. Sections 3-6 are particularly pertinent:

3. Actually God, who from all eternity regards Mary with a most favorable and unique affection, has "when the fullness of time came" put the plan of his providence into effect in such a way that all the privileges and prerogatives he had granted to her in his sovereign generosity were to shine forth in her in a kind of perfect harmony. And, although the Church has always recognized this supreme generosity and the perfect harmony of graces and has daily studied them more and more throughout the course of the centuries, still it is in our own age that the privilege of the bodily Assumption into heaven of Mary, the Virgin Mother of God, has certainly shone forth more clearly.

4. That privilege has shone forth in new radiance since our predecessor of immortal memory, Pius IX, solemnly proclaimed the dogma of the loving Mother of God's Immaculate Conception. These two privileges are most closely bound to one another. Christ overcame sin and death by his own death, and one who through Baptism has been born again in a supernatural way has conquered sin and death through the same Christ. Yet, according to the general rule, God does not will to grant to the just the full effect of the victory over death until the end of time has come. And so it is that the bodies of even the just are corrupted after death, and only on the last day will they be joined, each to its own glorious soul.

5. Now God has willed that the Blessed Virgin Mary should be exempted from this general rule. She, by an entirely unique privilege, completely overcame sin by her Immaculate Conception, and as a result she was not subject to the law of remaining in the corruption of the grave, and she did not have to wait until the end of time for the redemption of her body.

6. Thus, when it was solemnly proclaimed that Mary, the Virgin Mother of God, was from the very beginning free from the taint of original sin, the minds of the faithful were filled with a stronger hope that the day might soon come when the dogma of the Virgin Mary's bodily Assumption into heaven would also be defined by the Church's supreme teaching authority.[8]

Pope Pius XII made it very clear that the Assumption is an integral part of Catholic Dogma:

Hence if anyone, which God forbid, should dare willfully to deny or to call into doubt that which we have defined, let him know that he has fallen away completely from the divine and Catholic Faith.[9]

The bodily assumption of the Virgin Mary into heaven follows from her Immaculate Conception. For centuries before Pius IX declared the Immaculate Conception as dogma and Pius XII declared the Assumption, they were held as so by the Church. The writings of St. Louis de Montfort had already proclaimed both the

Immaculate Conception and the Assumption, and he observed that the Assumption was an intimate consequence of the Immaculate Conception. De Montfort asserted this nearly a century before the Immaculate Conception was declared as dogma and some two centuries before the Assumption was officially declared as dogma. There are plenty of opportunities for confusion about our Mother Mary that are passed on through formal and informal channels. Consider that if the Assumption is not an accepted part of Sister's treasury of faith, how realistic is it to expect her to have a devotion to the Rosary, given that the fourth Glorious Mystery is the Assumption of Mary, body and soul, into heaven?

Meditation - Catholic Style

The type of meditation that the Rosary requires is focusing one's thoughts; it is not the absence of thought, as Eastern spiritual methods espouse. Try this visualization: imagine your thoughts as emanating from your mind as rays of a flashlight. In meditation, we gather up those rays and focus them into a laser beam toward a particular target.

When we pray the Rosary, the target for each decade is the particular mystery of our meditation. For example, when praying the Sorrowful Mysteries, we focus our thoughts on Christ's Agony in the Garden during the first decade. I have found that beautiful religious art and Scripture have helped me to refocus my thoughts from a flashlight to a laser.

Many Catholics have never learned the ancient practice of *lectio divina* which is a great help in enhancing one's prayer life. Traditionally the method consists of four parts: reading the Scripture slowly, meditating on the Scripture, praying over the Scripture, and contemplating the Scripture. A fifth part, resolution or *resolutio*, was suggested recently in Tim Gray's book, *Praying Scripture for a Change*.[10]

Lectio divina requires a quiet place and an unhurried pace, both of which we must intentionally seek out and strive for in our daily lives—at least for the short time it takes to pray a Rosary. My favorite definition of *lectio divina* is taken directly from the companion materials of a course that I facilitated not so long ago on this subject:

Sacred Reading of the Scriptures (Lectio): The reading and rereading of the Scripture passage, paying close attention to words, details, themes, and patterns that speak to you.

Meditation (Meditatio): Meditating or reflecting on what you've read to gain understanding. Allow the Holy Spirit to guide you as you spend time pondering what you have read and striving to understand it in meditation.

Prayer (Oratio): A time to bring your meditative thoughts to God in prayer. Speak with God about how the connections and implications of your meditation on the Scripture affect your life and the lives of those around you.

Contemplation (Contemplatio): A time of quiet and rest, we listen and await God's voice. Contemplation allows one to enter decisively and more deeply into the Mystery of God—this is no small endeavor, so be patient as you engage this step and strive to be receptive to God's voice speaking into your life.[11]

Although the words meditation and contemplation are commonly used interchangeably, they are quite different in *lectio divina*. In meditation, one fully engages one's mind in analyzing the Scripture—one ponders and beholds. Alternatively, contemplation is an effortless entry into a rare space of heavenly delight but not by our efforts. It is a special place that the grace of God may lead up to from our spontaneous prayers of the heart (the *oratio* stage). There are no guarantees that one will ascend to *contemplatio*.

Lectio divina has a long tradition in the Catholic Church as a method of studying and praying with Scripture.[12] Guigo II, a Carthusian monk who lived in the 12th century, formalized the method. He is known for writing the book, *The Ladder of Monks*.

I was taught to think of the *lectio divina* method as a ladder. One always begins at the bottom rung of the ladder with *lectio* or a reading of Scripture. This is followed by *meditatio* or a mental pondering—the second rung. The *oratio* part (or third rung) is a spontaneous element that may occur. And when it does, we have a conversation topic with God through the leading of the Holy Spirit. One does not need to force *oratio*.

In our prayer life, if we start at the *oratio* stage, we may get bored "talking to" God because we run out of things to say. A conversation is two-way. The Scripture is God speaking to us. In *oratio* we respond to His topic of conversation. If nothing comes to mind, then one can go back to reading the next part of the Scripture and "climb up" again. In the apostolic letter, *Rosarium Virginis Mariae*, St. John Paul II draws a distinct contrast between *lectio divina* and praying the Rosary. He writes that praying the Rosary is no substitute for traditional *lectio divina* but rather the Rosary presupposes *lectio divina*. He writes,

> *Yet, even though the mysteries contemplated in the Rosary, even with the addition of the* mysteria lucis *[luminous mysteries], do no more than outline the fundamental elements of the life of Christ, they easily draw the mind to a more expansive reflection on the rest of the Gospel, especially when the Rosary is prayed in a setting of prolonged recollection.*[13]

In the same apostolic letter, St. John Paul II writes,

> *In order to supply a biblical foundation and greater depth to our meditation, it is helpful to follow the announcement of the mystery with the proclamation of a related biblical passage, long or short, depending on the circumstances. No other words can ever match the efficacy of the inspired word. As we listen, we are certain that this is the word of God, spoken for today and spoken "for me."*

> *If received in this way, the word of God can become part of the Rosary's methodology of repetition without giving rise to the ennui derived from the simple recollection of something already well known. It is not a matter of recalling information but of allowing God to speak. In certain solemn communal celebrations, this word can be appropriately illustrated by a brief commentary.*[14]

In subsequent chapters, I provide Scriptures for each bead of the rosary. Those Scriptures form the *lectio-like* bedrock of my meditations as I pray my Rosary. This Scripture-drenched method has removed any sense of drudgery (or ennui) associated with praying the Rosary for me. Occasionally I pause during my Rosary to enter into the spontaneous (or *oratio-like*) prayer stage briefly. I do not expect the Rosary to catapult me into *contemplatio*. But if it

29

did, then indeed I would have received an excellent and uncommon grace!

Returning once again to the opening scene of the "Dirty Santa" gift exchange...I did not steal the rosary beads from my Baptist friend though I had ample opportunity and wanted to do so. Now I pray that someday the hands used to unwrap the rosary will use the beads for their intended purpose.

CHAPTER 5

THE HARVEST:
MY JOURNEY TO THE ROSARY

When you say your Rosary the angels rejoice, The Blessed Trinity delights in it, my Son finds joy in it, too, and I myself am happier than you can possibly guess.[1]

~ Virgin Mary to Bl. Alan de Roche

My adoptive mother rarely spoke about her childhood, and only then if I insisted. She lived out the bulk of those years in an orphanage run by the Sisters of St. Joseph of Carondelet, three hours due east from where I spent my childhood. I don't recall that Mom ever spoke to me about her Catholic faith. I never saw her read the Bible or read any book, for that matter. Now I assume that she was just too busy.

She took in ironing, for a dollar an hour, to ensure that our little family had money for luxuries like an occasional hot lunch at school or a ticket to the movies with our childhood friends. The ironing money also helped when Dad had to quit working altogether from emphysema when my only sibling and I were in elementary school.

In exchange for our parochial school tuition, Mom cooked dinner at the convent which was home for the Sisters of St. Joseph of Carondelet, who taught at the only Catholic school in our small town. Back in those days, most Catholic parents sent their children to Catholic school regardless of the sacrifice they had to make. Mom and I attended Mass every Sunday and Holy Day of

Obligation, even when no one else in the family went with us.

Dad died ten years before Mom. Mom died when I was in my thirties. I had the responsibility of arranging her funeral and disposing of her simple earthly possessions. As I was stripping her bed for the last time to ready her single-wide trailer for sale, there they were, tucked between the sheets—her rosary beads.

I never thought much about Mom's faith. But as I looked upon her rosary, I imagined her fingers sliding over the beads, keeping rhythm with her prayers when she couldn't sleep. Pain was her constant bedtime companion, and I knew that she lay awake often during the night.

I had not said the Rosary since my Catholic school days, and like most things Catholic, it held no attraction for me when I was in my thirties. But the unspoken testimony of Mom's faith by the silent witness of her rosary beads remains sharply etched in my memory to this day.

Like many of my generation, I was baptized, sacramentalized, and catechized, but I was not evangelized. I had not given my heart to Christ in the deepest, most intimate of personal relationships. I had not journeyed to that sacred place from which there truly is no turning back, and from which springs joyful obedience to God's commandments—at any cost.

Twelve years after Mom died, I received the gift of faith in a most extraordinary manner—but that story is for another book. From the time of my conversion experience to the present day, my Bible, which I view as God's love letter to me, has been my most fascinating "friend." During the first year of my conversion, I read my Bible cover to cover, three times, spending anywhere from 30 to 45 minutes a day inhaling the words. The fantastic good news of the Gospel and the beauty of Salvation History captivated me and took root in my heart.

For the next ten years, I was one of the many ex-Catholics that swell the ranks of Evangelical Protestants. I gave no thought to the Rosary, but if I had, it would have been with a great sigh of relief, as the Rosary represented only monotony and repetition to me. Gleefully, I felt that the admonition in Matthew 6:7,

When you pray, don't babble on and on as the Gentiles do. They think their prayers are answered merely by repeating their words again and again. (NLT)[2]

was an absolution of my ever struggling to pray the Rosary again. I remember thinking, "Why do Catholics pray the Rosary when the Bible tells us not to keep repeating ourselves?"

I now recognize that I had a two-fold error in my thinking. I was taking the verse completely out of the historical context by not realizing that in biblical times, the pagans did babble nonsensical words as a form of prayer to false gods. Moreover, I had not ever learned how to meditate on the Mysteries of the Rosary.

Pope Paul VI confirmed the importance of meditation in his apostolic exhortation, *Marialis Cultus*, in 1974:

> *There has also been felt with greater urgency the need to point out once more the importance of a further essential element in the Rosary, in addition to the value of the elements of praise and petition, namely the element of contemplation. Without this the Rosary is a body without a soul, and its recitation is in danger of becoming a mechanical repetition of formulas and of going counter to the warning of Christ: "And in praying do not heap up empty phrases as the Gentiles do; for they think that they will be heard for their many words" (Mt. 6:7). By its nature the recitation of the Rosary calls for a quiet rhythm and a lingering pace, helping the individual to meditate on the mysteries of the Lord's life as seen through the eyes of her who was closest to the Lord. In this way, the unfathomable riches of these mysteries are unfolded.*[3]

Eventually, my hunger for the truth, obedience to an insistent internal prompting, and desire for deeper intimacy with God led me back to the Catholic Church. I discovered confirmation of the teachings of the Catholic Church in the writings of the early Church Fathers. The early Church Fathers either knew the apostles or were mentored by those within one or two generations of those who were trained by the apostles. I discovered rich avenues for spiritual growth in the writings of the saints that were primarily undiscovered or were being recreated in a rudimentary fashion by my favorite modern Protestant authors.

Shortly after returning to the Catholic Church, I read the book, *33 Days to Morning Glory*.[4] That book helped correct so many of the erroneous Marian ideas that I had picked up in the years between my conversion experience and my return to the Catholic

Church. After re-reading the book some months later and eventually facilitating a small group in my parish, I consecrated myself to Jesus through the Immaculate Heart of Mary. I want to explain what this consecration is because it profoundly impacted my life and that of my family.

If the concept of Marian Consecration is new to you, rest assured that it is Christocentric and, in no way, diminishes one's love for or worship of God. It is a process of detaching and abandoning of one's entire self and any merits from our prayers or actions into the hands of Mary. Marian Consecration is total trust that our Mother Mary will protect us spiritually and lead us to her Son in this life in the most direct way possible. One allows Mary the right to distribute the fruits of our prayers and sacrifices as she sees fit to the greatest good of mankind.

It may sound crazy to stand before the Lord at one's personal judgment empty-handed, but we are not alone, as Mary will be with us and covering us with the mantle of her merits. We trade our merits for hers. My personal experience leads me to believe that Marian Consecration is the single most important decision that an individual (or an entire parish) can make to fall more deeply in love with God and transform ourselves into the image of Christ.

I had been back in the full graces of the Catholic Church for about two years when I decided to pray the Rosary. Praying the Sorrowful Mysteries of the Rosary became my self-imposed penance on Friday, and this was only after I realized that Catholics were still obliged to do something special every Friday.[5] Only with tremendous effort did I will myself to pray the Rosary. My mind would seamlessly meander from concentrating on a particular mystery, such as the *Agony in the Garden*, to the evening's dinner menu or checking items off my to-do list or anything—anything but the mystery at hand.

Why was it so hard for me to look forward to praying the Rosary? By now, I knew many people who loved to pray it. Mary has implored us to pray the Rosary during so many of her apparitions. Since I had consecrated myself to Jesus through her Immaculate Heart, I persisted in my efforts to pray the Rosary for my Mother Mary's sake. But praying it still felt like torture. It was not something I looked forward to on Fridays.

I did take encouragement in the knowledge that great saints had struggles in their prayer life. So why should a spiritual weakling, such as myself, expect no challenges? For example, St. Teresa of Avila wrote much about her struggles in her prayer life, yet for what do we remember St. Teresa? We remember her for her great prayer life! After years of slogging through difficult periods of prayer, she was given the gift of contemplation, with the Lord lifting her up both spiritually and physically in ecstasy during prayer!

I facilitated the remainder of the Hearts Afire Parish-based Retreat Program (HAPP) at my home parish using the two studies: *Consoling the Heart of Jesus* and *Wisdom and Works of Mercy.*[6] Each retreat seemed better than the last. Not only did the retreat program help me fall in love with my Catholic faith and motivate me to become a saint, but it also started me on the path of pondering, among other things, the Rosary as a devotion. In one of the video segments of HAPP, Fr. Michael Gaitley asserts,

I don't know why Mary likes us to pray the Rosary so much, but she does!

Perhaps many people simply shrugged off Fr. Gaitley's exclamation, but it commanded a good portion of my thoughts for months. One day I got an answer, although I did not fully understand it at the time. I visualized myself with Mary during Jesus's Passion. My presence was indeed consoling Jesus. And I was in some way keeping Him company in Gethsemane when the other apostles could not stay awake. During the *Agony in the Garden*, three times Jesus implored his closest friends, Peter, James, and John, to stay awake and pray with him, but they kept falling asleep. His agony was so intense that his sweat became as drops of blood, a real medical phenomenon called hematidrosis. By praying and meditating on the first decade of the Sorrowful Mysteries, we keep watch with Jesus in his agony.

By "stitching" together ideas, all of which are taken from Fr. Michael Gaitley's HAPP sessions and books, I came up with an explanation that was consistent with my visualization.

1. God is outside of time and space. Clearly, He must be, as He created both space and time. Thus he cannot be contained by those dimensions.

2. Christ is fully divine and fully human. The Incarnation is this great mystery, second only to the mystery of the Trinity.

3. Events that Christ participated in between his human conception and his Ascension into heaven occurred in time and space, as do our actions. But Christ's actions, unlike our own, also exist outside of time and space as God-events.[7]

4. We can participate in events that exist outside of time in a special way when we meditate on the Mysteries of the Rosary because those are all God-events which exist in eternity, and are somehow ever-present, outside of space-time.

5. Mary wants us to pray the Rosary so that we can walk alongside with her as these events take place and so that, especially in the Sorrowful Mysteries, we can comfort Jesus and keep watch with Him. Recall how Jesus pleaded with his three closest friends to stay awake to keep him company for at least one hour in the Garden of Gethsemane. (See Mk 14:37).

The same God-event principle holds in the celebration of the Mass. We are united with the sacrifice of Calvary precisely because this God-event is outside of time yet ever-present in eternity. That is what it means to characterize the Mass as the re-presentation of the sacrifice of Calvary.

So let's think through the Joyful, Sorrowful, Glorious, and Luminous Mysteries. Are they *really* all God-events, which means that although they took place in space-time, the events of the Mysteries of the Rosary are eternally present?

If Jesus is present, then the event is a God-event, given His inseparable divine and human natures. Jesus is present in Mary's womb during the Annunciation and the Visitation because of Mary's "Yes" to the angel Gabriel.

The remainder of the Joyful Mysteries, certainly all the Sorrowful and Luminous Mysteries, and the first two Glorious Mysteries are God-events because Jesus is center stage. These are all God-events because Christ was present in time as a man but also as God outside of time, which we call eternity. For God, eternity has no beginning or end.

Now consider the last three Glorious Mysteries. We know that the third person of the Trinity was present at Pentecost, but does that make it a God-event? Here we must generalize a God-event to include the Trinity. "The Trinity is the greatest Mystery of the Christian Faith; it is the mystery of one God in three distinct Persons: Father, Son, and Holy Spirit. The revealed truth of the Holy Trinity is at the very root of the Church's living faith as expressed in the Creed. The mystery of the Trinity in itself is inaccessible to the human mind and is the object of faith only because it was revealed by Jesus Christ, the divine Son of the eternal Father."[8]

Since God created space and time, if any "person" of the Trinity enters space-time, then we have a God-event. So if the Holy Spirit or God the Father is present, that also qualifies as a God-event. That would certainly cover the third Glorious Mystery, Pentecost, but what about the Assumption of Mary and the Crowning of Mary? How can those be God-events? Mary is not God.

Mary, the Immaculate Conception, is the most perfect of all human creatures, so blessed as to have received the fruits of Christ's redemption at her conception, because she had to be redeemed like the rest of us. In Mary's Assumption, she was lifted body and soul into the presence of God—into heaven. Moreover, God has recognized her special status as the Mother of God by crowning her Queen of Heaven. So these are, in fact, God-events.

As we mathematicians like to say, QED, the abbreviation of the Latin phrase *quod erat demonstrandum,* meaning "which is what had to be shown" or "thus it has been demonstrated."

Now fast-forward to the Crucifixion. When we meditate on this Sorrowful Mystery, we can stay at the foot of the cross with His mother Mary, his Aunt Mary, John, and Mary Magdalene. Mother Mary wants us to comfort her son by uniting ourselves to these God-events. We can comfort Jesus by being with Him as we meditate during our Rosary because the mysteries are God-events that exist in eternity outside of space-time.

Once I realized that I could unite myself to Christ and console Him during His Passion—indeed that I can be there at Gethsemane and Calvary—my relationship with the Rosary changed entirely. Mary's Rosary is a sweet way of bringing me with her into the company of her Son. This is what it means to me when I *console the Heart of Jesus.*[9] No wonder St. Dominic had such success converting the Albigensians once Mary told him to "preach the Rosary!"[10]

Now that I understood the power of the Rosary, that left only one hurdle—getting my meditations on track. That is where *lectio divina* came to the rescue.

Previously, I had found that applying *lectio divina* to my daily scripture readings increased the quality of my prayer time tremendously as well as my ability to stay focused—I could pray from the heart more spontaneously and joyously. By using the method of *lectio divina* to pray with Scripture, my "monkey-jumping-from-tree-to-tree" mind could have laser focus. *Lectio divina* opened up my prayer life significantly and, I believe, helped me develop meditative skills to cultivate my rosary devotion.

One Friday afternoon while preparing to pray the Rosary inside my local Catholic Church, I discovered that I had left my tiny rosary meditation booklet at home. I conducted an online search with my smart phone with the hope that I might find something similar to use as a meditation aid. That online query led me to the *Sorrowful Mysteries of the Rosary for Justice* on the USCCB website.[11]

For several weeks I prayed my Rosary using those exact Scripture verses. I found that I could vocalize the prayers of the Rosary, while my eyes (and mind) focused (meditated) on the paired Scripture verses. My fingers could glide across each corresponding bead—which was a good thing because I could lose my count in my meditations. I have found this method of meditation has made my time of praying the Rosary not only fly by but is something that I look forward to each day.

I have created my scriptural Rosary for the Joyful, Sorrowful, Glorious and Luminous Mysteries. I have included St. Louis De Monfort's prayers at the end and beginning of each decade.

You will have to experiment to see what works best for you. Although I am quite able to meditate on the Scripture verses while simultaneously "vocalizing" the *Our Fathers*, *Hail Marys*, and *Glory Bes*, you can certainly pray the Scripture verse before or after you say the prayer for each rosary bead.

When I meditate using this method, my meditations can be so

vivid that I sometimes feel as if I am walking alongside Jesus holding Mary's hand. Finally, I can unite myself to the most sacred events in Salvation History through the holy Rosary.

Bead by Bead: The Scriptural Rosary

40

CHAPTER 6

JOYFUL MYSTERIES

St. John Paul II suggested praying the Joyful Mysteries on Monday and Saturday. However, during the Christmas season, we pray the Joyful Mysteries on Sunday instead of the Glorious Mysteries. The five Joyful Mysteries are:

- The Annunciation of Our Lord
- The Visitation
- The Nativity of Jesus
- The Presentation in the Temple
- The Finding in the Temple

Introductory Prayers

Sign of the Cross...

Prayer of Unity: "I unite myself with all the Saints in Heaven, and with all the just on earth; I unite myself with Thee, my Jesus, in order to praise Thy Holy Mother worthily and to praise Thee in her and by her. I renounce all the distractions that may come to me while I am saying this Rosary which I wish to say with modesty, attention, and devotion, just as if it were to be the last of my life."[1]

Petition: "We offer Thee, O most Holy Trinity, this Creed in honor of all the mysteries of our faith, this Our Father and these three Hail Marys in honor of the unity of Thy Essence and the

41

Trinity of Thy Persons. We ask of Thee a lively faith, a firm hope and an ardent charity. Amen."[2]

Apostles' Creed... Let the words of my mouth and the meditation of my heart be acceptable to you, O LORD, my rock and my redeemer. (Ps 19:14, NRSV)

Our Father... Make a joyful noise to the LORD, all the earth. Worship the LORD with gladness; come into his presence with singing. (Ps 100:1-2, NRSV)

Hail Mary... O come, let us sing to the LORD; let us make a joyful noise to the rock of our salvation! Let us come into his presence with thanksgiving; let us make a joyful noise to him with songs of praise! (Ps 95:1-2, NRSV)

Hail Mary... You show me the path of life. In your presence there is fullness of joy; in your right hand are pleasures forevermore. (Ps 16:11, NRSV)

Hail Mary... O sing to the LORD a new song, for he has done marvelous things. His right hand and his holy arm have gotten him victory. (Ps 98:1, NRSV)

Glory Be... May the God of hope fill you with all joy and peace in believing, so that you may abound in hope by the power of the Holy Spirit. (Rom 15:13, NRSV)

First Joyful Mystery: The Annunciation of Our Lord

Petition: "We offer Thee, O Lord Jesus, this [...] decade in honor of Thy Incarnation and we ask of Thee through this mystery and through the intercession of Thy Holy Mother, a profound humility."[3]

Setting: In the sixth month the angel Gabriel was sent by God to a town in Galilee called Nazareth, to a virgin engaged to a man whose name was Joseph, of the house of David. The virgin's name was Mary. (Lk 1:26-27, NRSV)

Our Father... And he came to her and said, "Greetings, favored one! The Lord is with you." (Lk 1:28, NRSV)

Hail Mary... But she was much perplexed by his words and pondered what sort of greeting this might be. (Lk 1:29, NRSV)

Hail Mary... The angel said to her, "Do not be afraid, Mary, for you have found favor with God. (Lk 1:30, NRSV)

Hail Mary... And now, you will conceive in your womb and bear a son, and you will name him Jesus. (Lk 1:31, NRSV)

Hail Mary... He will be great, and will be called the Son of the Most High, and the Lord God will give to him the throne of his ancestor David. He will reign over the house of Jacob forever, and of his kingdom there will be no end." (Lk 1:32-33, NRSV)

Hail Mary... Mary said to the angel, "How can this be, since I am a virgin?" (Lk 1:34, NRSV)

Hail Mary... The angel said to her, "The Holy Spirit will come upon you, and the power of the Most High will overshadow you; therefore the child to be born will be holy; he will be called Son of God. (Lk 1:35, NRSV)

Hail Mary... Then Mary said, "Here am I, the servant of the Lord; let it be with me according to your word." Then the angel departed from her. (Lk 1:38, NRSV)

Hail Mary... Her husband Joseph, being a righteous man and unwilling to expose her to public disgrace, planned to dismiss her quietly. (Mt 1:19, NRSV)

Hail Mary... But just when he had resolved to do this, an angel of the Lord appeared to him in a dream (Mt 1:20a, NRSV)

Fresco of Annunciation / Karl von Blaas / Altlerchenfelder Church, Vienna /
© Renata Sedmakova / Shutterstock.com

Hail Mary... and said, "Joseph, son of David, do not be afraid to take Mary as your wife, for the child conceived in her is from the Holy Spirit." (Mt 1:20b, NRSV)

Glory Be... When Joseph awoke from sleep, he did as the angel of the Lord commanded him; he took her as his wife, (Mt 1:24, NRSV)

Fatima Prayer... O my Jesus, forgive us our sins, save us from the fires of hell, and lead all souls to Heaven, especially those in most need of Thy Mercy.

End of Decade: "Grace of the mystery of the Incarnation, come down into my soul and make it truly humble."[4]

Second Joyful Mystery: The Visitation

Petition: "We offer Thee, O Lord Jesus, this [...] decade in honor of the Visitation of Thy Holy Mother to her cousin Saint Elizabeth, and we ask of Thee through this mystery and through Mary's intercession, a perfect charity towards our neighbor."[5]

Setting: And now, your relative Elizabeth in her old age has also conceived a son; and this is the sixth month for her who was said to be barren. For nothing will be impossible with God." (Lk 1:36-37, NRSV)

Our Father... In those days Mary set out and went with haste to a Judean town in the hill country, where she entered the house of Zechariah and greeted Elizabeth. (Lk 1:39-40, NRSV)

Hail Mary... When Elizabeth heard Mary's greeting, the child leaped in her womb. (Lk 1:41a, NRSV)

Hail Mary... And Elizabeth was filled with the Holy Spirit and exclaimed with a loud cry, "Blessed are you among women, and blessed is the fruit of your womb. (Lk 1:41b-42, NRSV)

Visitation of the Virgin Mary / St-Etienne-du-Mont Church, Paris /
© Zvonimir Atletic / Shutterstock.com

Hail Mary... And why has this happened to me, that the mother of my Lord comes to me? (Lk 1:43, NRSV)

Hail Mary... For as soon as I heard the sound of your greeting, the child in my womb leaped for joy. (Lk 1:44, NRSV)

Hail Mary... And blessed is she who believed that there would be a fulfillment of what was spoken to her by the Lord." (Lk 1:45, NRSV)

Hail Mary... And Mary said, "My soul magnifies the Lord, and my spirit rejoices in God my Savior, (Lk 1:46-47, NRSV)

Hail Mary... for he has looked with favor on the lowliness of his servant. Surely, from now on all generations will call me blessed; (Lk 1:48, NRSV)

Hail Mary... for the Mighty One has done great things for me, and holy is his name. (Lk 1:49, NRSV)

Hail Mary... His mercy is for those who fear him from generation to generation. (Lk 1:50, NRSV)

Hail Mary... He has shown strength with his arm; he has scattered the proud in the thoughts of their hearts. (Lk 1:51, NRSV)

Glory Be... And Mary remained with her about three months and then returned to her home. (Lk 1:56, NRSV)

Fatima Prayer... O my Jesus, forgive us our sins, save us from the fires of hell, and lead all souls to Heaven, especially those in most need of Thy Mercy.

End of Decade: "Grace of the mystery of the Visitation come down into my soul and make it really charitable."[6]

Third Joyful Mystery: The Nativity of Jesus

Petition: "We offer Thee, O Child Jesus, this [...] decade in honor of Thy Blessed Nativity, and we ask of Thee, through this mystery and through the intercession of Thy Blessed Mother detachment from things of this world, love of poverty and love of the poor."[7]

Setting: In those days a decree went out from Emperor Augustus that all the world should be registered. This was the first registration and was taken while Quirinius was governor of Syria. All went to their own towns to be registered. (Lk 2:1-3, NRSV)

Our Father... Joseph also went from the town of Nazareth in Galilee to Judea, to the city of David called Bethlehem, because he was descended from the house and family of David. He went to be registered with Mary, to whom he was engaged and who was expecting a child. (Lk 2:4-5, NRSV)

Hail Mary... "Look, the virgin shall conceive and bear a son, and they shall name him Emmanuel," which means, "God is with us." (Mt 1:23, NRSV)

Hail Mary... While they were there, the time came for her to deliver her child. And she gave birth to her firstborn son (Lk 2:6-7a, NRSV)

Hail Mary... and wrapped him in bands of cloth, and laid him in a manger, because there was no place for them in the inn. (Lk 2:7b, NRSV)

Hail Mary... In that region there were shepherds living in the fields, keeping watch over their flock by night. Then an angel of the Lord stood before them, and the glory of the Lord shone around them, (Lk 2:9a, NRSV)

Hail Mary... and they were terrified. But the angel said to them, "Do not be afraid; for see—I am bringing you good news of great joy for all the people: (Lk 2:9b-10, NRSV)

Adoration of the Shepherds / Gerrit van Honthorst / Florence, Italy / Scala / Art Resource, NY

Hail Mary... to you is born this day in the city of David a Savior, who is the Messiah, the Lord. (Lk 2:11, NRSV)

Hail Mary... And suddenly there was with the angel a multitude of the heavenly host, praising God (Lk 2:13, NRSV)

Hail Mary... [and saying,] "Glory to God in the highest heaven, and on earth peace among those whom he favors!" (Lk 2:14, NRSV)

Hail Mary... When the angels had left them and gone into heaven, the shepherds said to one another, "Let us go now to Bethlehem and see this thing that has taken place, which the Lord has made known to us." (Lk 2:15, NRSV)

Hail Mary... So they went with haste and found Mary and Joseph, and the child lying in the manger. When they saw this, they made known what had been told them about this child; (Lk 2:16-17, NRSV)

Glory Be... and all who heard it were amazed at what the shepherds told them. But Mary treasured all these words and pondered them in her heart. (Lk 2:18-19, NRSV)

Fatima Prayer... O my Jesus, forgive us our sins, save us from the fires of hell, and lead all souls to Heaven, especially those in most need of Thy Mercy.

End of Decade: "Grace of the mystery of the Nativity come down into my soul and make me truly poor in spirit."[8]

Fourth Joyful Mystery: The Presentation in the Temple

Petition: "We offer Thee, O Lord Jesus, this [...] decade in honor of Thy Presentation in the temple by the hands of Mary, and we ask of Thee, through this mystery and through the intercession of Thy Blessed Mother, the gift of wisdom and purity of heart and body."[9]

Setting: When the time came for their purification according to the law of Moses, they brought him up to Jerusalem to present him to the Lord (Lk 2:22, NRSV)

Our Father... (as it is written in the law of the Lord, "Every firstborn male shall be designated as holy to the Lord"), (Lk 2:23, NRSV)

Hail Mary... and they offered a sacrifice according to what is stated in the law of the Lord, "a pair of turtledoves or two young pigeons." (Lk 2:24, NRSV)

Hail Mary... Now there was a man in Jerusalem whose name was Simeon; this man was righteous and devout, looking forward to the consolation of Israel, and the Holy Spirit rested on him. (Lk 2:25, NRSV)

Hail Mary... It had been revealed to him by the Holy Spirit that he would not see death before he had seen the Lord's Messiah. (Lk 2:26, NRSV)

Hail Mary... Guided by the Spirit, Simeon came into the temple; and when the parents brought in the child Jesus, to do for him what was customary under the law, (Lk 2:27, NRSV)

Hail Mary... "Master, now you are dismissing your servant in peace, according to your word; for my eyes have seen your salvation, (Lk 2:29-30, NRSV)

Hail Mary... which you have prepared in the presence of all peoples, for my eyes have seen your salvation, a light for revelation to the Gentiles and for glory to your people Israel." (Lk 2:31-32, NRSV)

Hail Mary... Then Simeon blessed them and said to his mother Mary, "This child is destined for the falling and the rising of many in Israel, and to be a sign that will be opposed (Lk 2:34, NRSV)

The Presentation of Jesus at the Temple / St. Marcus Monastery, Florence /
© Ana Tramont / shutterstock.com

Hail Mary... so that the inner thoughts of many will be revealed—
and a sword will pierce your own soul too." (Lk 2:35, NRSV)

Hail Mary... There was also a prophet, Anna the daughter of
Phanuel, of the tribe of Asher. She was of a great age, having lived
with her husband seven years after her marriage, (Lk 2:36, NRSV)

Hail Mary... then as a widow to the age of eighty-four. She never
left the temple but worshiped there with fasting and prayer night
and day. (Lk 2:37, NRSV)

Glory Be... At that moment she came, and began to praise God
and to speak about the child to all who were looking for the
redemption of Jerusalem. (Lk 2:38, NRSV)

Fatima Prayer... O my Jesus, forgive us our sins, save us from the fires of hell, and lead all souls to Heaven, especially those in most need of Thy Mercy.

End of Decade: "Grace of the mystery of the Purification, come down into my soul and make it really wise and really pure."[10]

Fifth Joyful Mystery: The Finding in the Temple

Petition: "We offer Thee, O Lord Jesus, this [...] decade in honor of Thy Finding in the Temple among the learned men by Our Lady, after she had lost Thee, and we ask Thee, through this mystery and through the intercession of Thy Blessed Mother, to convert us and help us amend our lives, and also to convert all sinners [...]."[11]

Setting: Now every year his parents went to Jerusalem for the festival of the Passover. And when he was twelve years old, they went up as usual for the festival. (Lk 2:41-42, NRSV)

Our Father... When the festival was ended and they started to return, the boy Jesus stayed behind in Jerusalem, but his parents did not know it. (Lk 2:43, NRSV)

Hail Mary... Assuming that he was in the group of travelers, they went a day's journey. Then they started to look for him among their relatives and friends. (Lk 2:44, NRSV)

Hail Mary... When they did not find him, they returned to Jerusalem to search for him. (Lk 2:45, NRSV)

Hail Mary... After three days they found him in the temple, sitting among the teachers, listening to them and asking them questions. And all who heard him were amazed at his understanding and his answers. (Lk 2:46-47, NRSV)

*Twelve Year Old Christ in the Temple / Heinrich Hofmann / Hamburger Kunsthalle,
Hamburg / bpk Bildagentur / Art Resource, NY*

Hail Mary... When his parents saw him they were astonished; and
his mother said to him, "Child, why have you treated us like this?
Look, your father and I have been searching for you in great
anxiety." (Lk 2:48, NRSV)

Hail Mary... He said to them, "Why were you searching for me?
Did you not know that I must be in my Father's house?" (Lk 2:49,
NRSV)

Hail Mary... But they did not understand what he said to them.
(Lk 2:50, NRSV)

Hail Mary... Then he went down with them and came to
Nazareth, and was obedient to them. His mother treasured all these
things in her heart. (Lk 2:51, NRSV)

Hail Mary... And Jesus increased in wisdom and in years, and in
divine and human favor. (Lk 2:52, NRSV)

Hail Mary... The spirit of the LORD shall rest on him, the spirit of wisdom and understanding, (Is 11:2a, NRSV)

Hail Mary... the spirit of counsel and might, the spirit of knowledge and the fear of the LORD. (Is 11:2b, NRSV)

Glory Be... A shoot shall come out from the stump of Jesse, and a branch shall grow out of his roots. (Is 11:1, NRSV)

Fatima Prayer... O my Jesus, forgive us our sins, save us from the fires of hell, and lead all souls to Heaven, especially those in most need of Thy Mercy.

End of Decade: "Grace of the mystery of the Finding of the Child Jesus in the Temple, come down into my soul and truly convert me."[12]

Hail, Holy Queen... Hail, holy Queen, Mother of mercy, our life, our sweetness and our hope. To thee do we cry, poor banished children of Eve. To thee do we send up our sighs, mourning and weeping in this valley of tears. Turn then, most gracious Advocate, thine eyes of mercy toward us, and after this our exile, show unto us the blessed fruit of thy womb, Jesus. O clement, O loving, O sweet Virgin Mary. Pray for us, O Holy Mother of God. That we may be made worthy of the promises of Christ. Amen.

Concluding Prayer... "We beseech Thee, dear Lord Jesus by the [...] mysteries of Thy life, passion and death, by Thy glory and by the merits of Thy Blessed Mother, to convert sinners and help the dying, to deliver the Holy Souls from Purgatory and to give us all Thy grace so that we may live well and die well—and please give us the Light of Thy Glory later on so that we may see Thee face to face and love Thee for all eternity. Amen. So be it."[13]

Bead by Bead: The Scriptural Rosary

56

CHAPTER 7

SORROWFUL MYSTERIES

St. John Paul II suggested praying the Sorrowful Mysteries on Tuesday and Friday. However, during the season of Lent, we pray the Sorrowful Mysteries on Sunday instead of the Glorious Mysteries. The five Sorrowful Mysteries are:

- The Agony in the Garden
- The Scourging at the Pillar
- The Crowning with Thorns
- The Carrying of the Cross
- The Crucifixion and Death

Introductory Prayers

Sign of the Cross...

Prayer of Unity: "I unite myself with all the Saints in Heaven, and with all the just on earth; I unite myself with Thee, my Jesus, in order to praise Thy Holy Mother worthily and to praise Thee in her and by her. I renounce all the distractions that may come to me while I am saying this Rosary which I wish to say with modesty, attention, and devotion, just as if it were to be the last of my life."[1]

Petition: "We offer Thee, O most Holy Trinity, this Creed in honor of all the mysteries of our faith, this Our Father and these three Hail Marys in honor of the unity of Thy Essence and the Trinity of Thy Persons. We ask of Thee a lively faith, a firm hope and an ardent charity. Amen."[2]

Apostles' Creed... He himself bore our sins in his body upon the cross, so that, free from sin, we might live for righteousness; by his wounds you have been healed. (1 Pt 2:24, NRSV)

Our Father... The righteous one, my servant, shall make many righteous, and he shall bear their iniquities. (Is 53:11b, NRSV)

Hail Mary... For the message about the cross is foolishness to those who are perishing, but to us who are being saved it is the power of God. (1 Cor 1:18, NRSV)

Hail Mary... Surely he has borne our infirmities and carried our diseases; yet we accounted him stricken, struck down by God, and afflicted. (Is 53:4, NRSV)

Hail Mary... who, though he was in the form of God, did not regard equality with God as something to be exploited, but emptied himself, taking the form of a slave, being born in human likeness. And being found in human form, (Phil 2:6-7, NRSV)

Glory Be... My God, my God, why have you forsaken me? Why are you so far from helping me, from the words of my groaning? (Ps 22:1, NRSV)

First Sorrowful Mystery: The Agony in the Garden

Petition: "We offer Thee, O Lord Jesus, this [...] decade in honor of Thy mortal Agony in the Garden of Olives and we ask of Thee, through this mystery and through the intercession of Thy Blessed Mother, perfect sorrow for our sins and the virtue of perfect obedience to Thy Holy Will."[3]

Setting: After Jesus had spoken these words, he went out with his disciples across the Kidron valley to a place where there was a garden, which he and his disciples entered. (Jn 18:1, NRSV)

Our Father... They went to a place called Gethsemane; and he said to his disciples, "Sit here while I pray." He took with him Peter and James and James and John, and began to be distressed and agitated. (Mk 14:32-33, NRSV)

Hail Mary... And he said to them, "I am deeply grieved, even to death; remain here, and keep awake." (Mk 14:34, NRSV)

Hail Mary... And going a little farther, he threw himself on the ground and prayed that, if it were possible, the hour might pass from him. (Mk 14:35, NRSV)

Hail Mary... He said, "Abba, Father, for you all things are possible; remove this cup from me; yet, not what I want, but what you want." (Mk 14:36, NRSV)

Agony in the Garden / Paolo Veronese / Pinacoteca di Brera / Scala / Art Resource, NY

Hail Mary... Then an angel from heaven appeared to him and gave him strength. (Lk 22:43, NRSV)

Hail Mary... In his anguish he prayed more earnestly, and his sweat became like great drops of blood falling down on the ground. (Lk 22:44, NRSV)

Hail Mary... He came and found them sleeping; and he said to Peter, "Simon, are you asleep? Could you not keep awake one hour? (Mk 14:37, NRSV)

Hail Mary... Keep awake and pray that you may not come into the time of trial; the spirit indeed is willing, but the flesh is weak." (Mk 14:38, NRSV)

Hail Mary... And again he went away and prayed, saying the same words. And once more he came and found them sleeping, for their eyes were very heavy; and they did not know what to say to him. (Mk 14:39-40, NRSV)

Hail Mary... So leaving them again, he went away and prayed for the third time, saying the same words. Then he came to the disciples and said to them, "Are you still sleeping and taking your rest? (Mt 26:44-45a, NRSV)

Hail Mary... While he was still speaking, suddenly a crowd came, and the one called Judas, one of the twelve, was leading them. He approached Jesus to kiss him; (Lk 22:47, NRSV)

Glory Be... but Jesus said to him, "Judas, is it with a kiss that you are betraying the Son of Man?" (Lk 22:48, NRSV)

Fatima Prayer... O my Jesus, forgive us our sins, save us from the fires of hell, and lead all souls to Heaven, especially those in most need of Thy Mercy.

End of Decade: "Grace of Our Lord's Agony, come down into my soul and make me truly contrite and perfectly Obedient to Thy will."[4]

Second Sorrowful Mystery: The Scourging at the Pillar

Petition: "We offer Thee, O Lord Jesus, this [...] decade in honor of Thy Bloody Scourging and we ask of Thee, through this mystery and through the intercession of Thy Blessed Mother, the grace to mortify our senses perfectly."⁵

Setting: As soon as it was morning, the chief priests held a consultation with the elders and scribes and the whole council. They bound Jesus, led him away, and handed him over to Pilate. (Mk 15:1, NRSV)

Our Father... Pilate asked him, "Are you the King of the Jews?" He answered him, "You say so." Then the chief priests accused him of many things. (Mk 15:2-3, NRSV)

Hail Mary... Pilate asked him again, "Have you no answer? See how many charges they bring against you." (Mk 15:4, NRSV)

Hail Mary... But Jesus made no further reply, so that Pilate was amazed. (Mk 15:5, NRSV)

Hail Mary... Now at the festival he used to release a prisoner for them, anyone for whom they asked. Now a man called Barabbas was in prison with the rebels who had committed murder during the insurrection. (Mk 15:6-7, NRSV)

Hail Mary... Then he answered them, "Do you want me to release for you the King of the Jews?" For he realized that it was out of jealousy that the chief priests had handed him over. (Mk 15:9-10, NRSV)

Hail Mary... While he was sitting on the judgment seat, his wife sent word to him, "Have nothing to do with that innocent man, for today I have suffered a great deal because of a dream about him." (Mt 27:19, NRSV)

Hail Mary... But the chief priests stirred up the crowd to have him release Barabbas for them instead. (Mk 15:11, NRSV)

Hail Mary... So when Pilate saw that he could do nothing, but rather that a riot was beginning, he took some water and washed his hands before the crowd, saying, "I am innocent of this man's blood; see to it yourselves." (Mt 27:24, NRSV)

*Flagellation of Christ / Leonardo Corona / San Giovanni in Bragora /
Cameraphoto Arte, Venice / Art Resource, NY*

Hail Mary... Then Pilate took Jesus and had him flogged. (Jn 19:1, NRSV)

Hail Mary... upon him was the punishment that made us whole, and by his bruises we are healed. (Is 53:5b, NRSV)

Hail Mary... Yet it was the will of the LORD to crush him with pain. When you make his life an offering for sin, (Is 53:10a, NRSV)

Glory Be... All we like sheep have gone astray; we have all turned to our own way, and the LORD has laid on him the iniquity of us all. (Is 53:6, NRSV)

Fatima Prayer... O my Jesus, forgive us our sins, save us from the fires of hell, and lead all souls to Heaven, especially those in most need of Thy Mercy.

End of Decade: "Grace of Our Lord's Scourging, come down into my soul and make me truly mortified."[6]

Third Sorrowful Mystery: The Crowning with Thorns

Petition: "We offer Thee, O Lord Jesus, this [...] decade in honor of Thy cruel crowning with thorns, and we ask of Thee, through this mystery and through the intercession of Thy Blessed Mother, a great contempt of the [godless ways and desires of this] world."[7]

Setting: Then the soldiers of the governor took Jesus into the governor's headquarters, and they gathered the whole cohort around him. (Mt 26:27, NRSV)

Our Father... And they clothed him in a purple cloak; and after twisting some thorns into a crown, they put it on him. (Mk 15:17, NRSV)

Hail Mary... And they began saluting him, "Hail, King of the Jews!" (Mk 15:18, NRSV)

Hail Mary... They struck his head with a reed, spat upon him, and knelt down in homage to him. (Mk 15:19, NRSV)

Hail Mary... He was oppressed, and he was afflicted, yet he did not open his mouth; (Is 53:7a, NRSV)

Hail Mary... like a lamb that is led to the slaughter, and like a sheep that before its shearers is silent, so he did not open his mouth. (Is 53:7b, NRSV)

Hail Mary... By a perversion of justice he was taken away. Who could have imagined his future? (Is 53:8a, NRSV)

Hail Mary... because he poured out himself to death, and was numbered with the transgressors; (Is 53:12b, NRSV)

Hail Mary... yet he bore the sin of many, and made intercession for the transgressors. (Is 53:12c, NRSV)

Hail Mary... Pilate went out again and said to them, "Look, I am bringing him out to you to let you know that I find no case against him." (Jn 19:4, NRSV)

Christ Crowned with Thorns / Hendrick Terbrugghen / Statens Museum, Copenhagen / HIP / Art Resource, NY

Hail Mary... So Jesus came out, wearing the crown of thorns and the purple robe. Pilate said to them, "Here is the man!" (Jn 19:5, NRSV)

Hail Mary... I gave my back to those who struck me, and my cheeks to those who pulled out the beard; I did not hide my face from insult and spitting. (Is 50:6, NRSV)

Glory Be... "Blessed are you when people revile you and persecute you and utter all kinds of evil against you falsely on my account. (Mt 5:11, NRSV)

Fatima Prayer... O my Jesus, forgive us our sins, save us from the fires of hell, and lead all souls to Heaven, especially those in most need of Thy Mercy.

End of Decade: "Grace of the mystery of Our Lord's crowning with Thorns, come down into my soul and make me despise the [godless ways and desires of this] world."[8]

Fourth Sorrowful Mystery: The Carrying of the Cross

Petition: "We offer Thee, O Lord Jesus, this [...] decade in honor of Thy carrying of Thy Cross and we ask of Thee, through this mystery and through the intercession of Thy Blessed Mother, to give us great patience in carrying our cross in Thy footsteps every day of our life."[9]

Setting: But they kept urgently demanding with loud shouts that he should be crucified; and their voices prevailed. So Pilate gave his verdict that their demand should be granted. (Lk 23:23-24, NRSV)

Our Father... He released the man they asked for, the one who had been put in prison for insurrection and murder, and he handed Jesus over as they wished. (Lk 23:25, NRSV)

Hail Mary... They compelled a passer-by, who was coming in from the country, to carry his cross; it was Simon of Cyrene, the father of Alexander and Rufus. (Mk 15:21, NRSV)

Hail Mary... they laid the cross on him, and made him carry it behind Jesus. (Lk 23:26b, NRSV)

Hail Mary... A great number of the people followed him, and among them were women who were beating their breasts and wailing for him. (Lk 23:27, NRSV)

Christ Falls on the Way to Calvary / Raphael / Museo Nacional del Prado / Art Resource, NY

Hail Mary... But Jesus turned to them and said, "Daughters of Jerusalem, do not weep for me, but weep for yourselves and for your children. (Lk 23:28, NRSV)

Hail Mary... For the days are surely coming when they will say,

'Blessed are the barren, and the wombs that never bore, and the breasts that never nursed.' (Lk 23:29, NRSV)

Hail Mary... Then he said to them all, "If any want to become my followers, let them deny themselves and take up their cross daily and follow me. (Lk 9:23, NRSV)

Hail Mary... O LORD, how many are my foes! Many are rising against me; many are saying to me, "There is no help for you in God." (Ps 3:1-2, NRSV)

Hail Mary... He was despised and rejected by others; a man of suffering and acquainted with infirmity; (Is 53:3a, NRSV)

Hail Mary... and as one from whom others hide their faces he was despised, and we held him of no account. (Is 53:3b, NRSV)

Hail Mary... Just as there were many who were astonished at him—so marred was his appearance, beyond human semblance, and his form beyond that of mortals— (Is 52:14, NRSV)

Glory Be... Whoever does not carry the cross and follow me cannot be my disciple. (Lk 14:27, NRSV)

Fatima Prayer... O my Jesus, forgive us our sins, save us from the fires of hell, and lead all souls to Heaven, especially those in most need of Thy Mercy.

End of Decade: "Grace of the mystery of carrying the Cross, come down into my soul and make me truly contrite and make me truly patient"[10]

Fifth Sorrowful Mystery: The Crucifixion

Petition: "We offer Thee, O Lord Jesus, this [...] decade in honor of Thy Crucifixion on Mount Calvary, and we ask of Thee, through this mystery and through the intercession of Thy Blessed Mother, a great horror of sin, a love of the Cross, and the grace of a holy death for us and for those who are now in their last agony."[11]

Setting: And when they came to a place called Golgotha (which means Place of a Skull), they offered him wine to drink, mixed with gall; but when he tasted it, he would not drink it. (Mt 27:33-34, NRSV)

Our Father... And when they had crucified him, they divided his clothes among themselves by casting lots; then they sat down there and kept watch over him. (Mt 27:35-36, NRSV)

Hail Mary... Those who passed by derided him, shaking their heads and saying, "You who would destroy the temple and build it in three days, save yourself! If you are the Son of God, come down from the cross." (Mt 27:39-40, NRSV)

Hail Mary... One of the criminals who were hanged there kept deriding him and saying, "Are you not the Messiah? Save yourself and us!" (Lk 23:39, NRSV)

Hail Mary... But the other rebuked him, saying, "Do you not fear God, since you are under the same sentence of condemnation? And we indeed have been condemned justly, for we are getting what we deserve for our deeds, but this man has done nothing wrong." (Lk 23:40-41, NRSV)

Hail Mary... Then he said, "Jesus, remember me when you come into your kingdom." He replied, "Truly I tell you, today you will be with me in Paradise." (Lk 23:42-43, NRSV)

Hail Mary... When Jesus saw his mother and the disciple whom he loved standing beside her, he said to his mother, "Woman, here is your son." Then he said to the disciple, "Here is your mother." And from that hour the disciple took her into his own home. (Jn 19:26-27, NRSV)

Hail Mary... It was now about noon, and darkness came over the whole land until three in the afternoon, while the sun's light failed; (Lk 23:44-45a, NRSV)

Jesus on the Cross / Rene de Cramer / St. Peter's Church, Gent, Belgium /
© Renata Sedmakova / Shutterstock.com

Hail Mary... And about three o'clock Jesus cried with a loud voice, "Eli, Eli, lema sabachthani?" that is, "My God, my God, why have you forsaken me?" (Mt 27:46, NRSV)

Hail Mary... After this, when Jesus knew that all was now finished, he said (in order to fulfill the scripture), "I am thirsty." A jar full of sour wine was standing there. So they put a sponge full of the wine on a branch of hyssop and held it to his mouth. When

Jesus had received the wine, he said, "It is finished." (Jn 19:28-30a, NRSV)

Hail Mary... Then Jesus, crying with a loud voice, said, "Father, into your hands I commend my spirit." Having said this, he breathed his last. (Lk 23:46, NRSV)

Hail Mary... At that moment the curtain of the temple was torn in two, from top to bottom. The earth shook, and the rocks were split. The tombs also were opened, and many bodies of the saints who had fallen asleep were raised. (Mt 27:51-52, NRSV)

Glory Be... Now when the centurion and those with him, who were keeping watch over Jesus, saw the earthquake and what took place, they were terrified and said, "Truly this man was God's Son!" (Mt 27:54, NRSV)

Fatima Prayer... O my Jesus, forgive us our sins, save us from the fires of hell, and lead all souls to Heaven, especially those in most need of Thy Mercy.

End of Decade: "Grace of the mystery of the Death and Passion of Our Lord and Savior Jesus Christ, come down into my soul and make me truly holy."[12]

Hail, Holy Queen... Hail, holy Queen, Mother of mercy, our life, our sweetness and our hope. To thee do we cry, poor banished children of Eve. To thee do we send up our sighs, mourning and weeping in this valley of tears. Turn then, most gracious Advocate, thine eyes of mercy toward us, and after this our exile, show unto us the blessed fruit of thy womb, Jesus. O clement, O loving, O sweet Virgin Mary. Pray for us, O Holy Mother of God. That we may be made worthy of the promises of Christ. Amen.

Concluding Prayer... "We beseech Thee, dear Lord Jesus by the [...] mysteries of Thy life, passion and death, by Thy glory and by the merits of Thy Blessed Mother, to convert sinners and help the dying, to deliver the Holy Souls from Purgatory and to give us all Thy grace so that we may live well and die well—and please give us the Light of Thy Glory later on so that we may see Thee face to face and love Thee for all eternity. Amen. So be it."[13]

The Crucifixion / Murillo / © The Metropolitan Museum of Art / Art Resource, NY

CHAPTER 8

GLORIOUS MYSTERIES

St. John Paul II suggested praying the Glorious Mysteries on Wednesday and Sunday. However, we pray the Joyful Mysteries on Sunday during the Christmas season, and the Sorrowful Mysteries on Sundays of Lent. The five Glorious Mysteries are:

- The Resurrection of our Lord
- The Ascension into Heaven
- The Descent of the Holy Spirit
- The Assumption of Mary
- The Coronation of Mary

Introductory Prayers

Sign of the Cross...

Prayer of Unity: "I unite myself with all the Saints in Heaven, and with all the just on earth; I unite myself with Thee, my Jesus, in order to praise Thy Holy Mother worthily and to praise Thee in her and by her. I renounce all the distractions that may come to me while I am saying this Rosary which I wish to say with modesty, attention, and devotion, just as if it were to be the last of my life."[1]

Petition: "We offer Thee, O most Holy Trinity, this Creed in honor of all the mysteries of our faith, this Our Father and these three Hail Marys in honor of the unity of Thy Essence and the Trinity of Thy Persons. We ask of Thee a lively faith, a firm hope and an ardent charity. Amen."[2]

Apostles' Creed... "Hallelujah! For the Lord our God the Almighty reigns. Let us rejoice and exult and give him the glory, (Rev 19:6b-7a, NRSV)

Our Father... Glory in his holy name; let the hearts of those who seek the LORD rejoice. Seek the LORD and his strength; seek his presence continually. (Ps 105:3-4, NRSV)

Hail Mary... On the glorious splendor of your majesty, and on your wondrous works, I will meditate. (Ps 145:5, NRSV)

Hail Mary... Be exalted, O God, above the heavens. Let your glory be over all the earth. (Ps 57:5, NRSV)

Hail Mary... I will sing to my God a new song: O Lord, you are great and glorious, wonderful in strength, invincible. (Jdt 16:13, NRSV)

Glory Be... to the only God our Savior, through Jesus Christ our Lord, be glory, majesty, power, and authority, before all time and now and forever. Amen. (Jude 1:25, NRSV)

First Glorious Mystery: The Resurrection of our Lord

Petition: "We offer Thee, O Lord Jesus, this [...] decade in honor of Thy triumphant Resurrection and we ask of Thee, through this mystery and through the intercession of Thy Blessed Mother, a lively faith."[3]

Setting: When the sabbath was over, Mary Magdalene, and Mary the mother of James, and Salome bought spices, so that they might go and anoint him. And very early on the first day of the week, when the sun had risen, they went to the tomb. (Mk 16:1-2, NRSV)

Our Father... They had been saying to one another, "Who will roll away the stone for us from the entrance to the tomb?" When they looked up, they saw that the stone, which was very large, had already been rolled back. (Mk 16:3-4, NRSV)

Hail Mary... As they entered the tomb, they saw a young man, dressed in a white robe, sitting on the right side; and they were alarmed. (Mk 16:5, NRSV)

Risen Christ and Madonna, with angels and saints / © fotogiunta / Shutterstock.com

Hail Mary... But he said to them, "Do not be alarmed; you are looking for Jesus of Nazareth, who was crucified. He has been raised; he is not here. Look, there is the place they laid him. (Mk 16:6, NRSV)

Hail Mary... But go, tell his disciples and Peter that he is going ahead of you to Galilee; there you will see him, just as he told you." (Mk 16:7, NRSV)

Hail Mary... So they went out and fled from the tomb, for terror and amazement had seized them; and they said nothing to anyone, for they were afraid. (Mk 16:8, NRSV)

Hail Mary... Now after he rose early on the first day of the week, he appeared first to Mary Magdalene, from whom he had cast out seven demons. (Mk 16:9, NRSV)

Hail Mary... Jesus said to her, "Woman, why are you weeping? Whom are you looking for?" Supposing him to be the gardener, she said to him, "Sir, if you have carried him away, tell me where you have laid him, and I will take him away." (Jn 20:15, NRSV)

Hail Mary... Jesus said to her, "Mary!" She turned and said to him in Hebrew, "Rabbouni!" (which means Teacher). (Jn 20:16, NRSV)

Hail Mary... Jesus said to her, "Do not hold on to me, because I have not yet ascended to the Father. But go to my brothers and say to them, 'I am ascending to my Father and your Father, to my God and your God.'" (Jn 20:17, NRSV)

Hail Mary... She went out and told those who had been with him, while they were mourning and weeping. But when they heard that he was alive and had been seen by her, they would not believe it. (Mk 16:10-11, NRSV)

Hail Mary... But Peter got up and ran to the tomb; stooping and looking in, he saw the linen cloths by themselves; then he went home, amazed at what had happened. (Lk 24:12, NRSV)

Glory Be... If the Spirit of him who raised Jesus from the dead dwells in you, he who raised Christ from the dead will give life to your mortal bodies also through his Spirit that dwells in you. (Rom 8:11, NRSV)

Fatima Prayer... O my Jesus, forgive us our sins, save us from the fires of hell, and lead all souls to Heaven, especially those in most need of Thy Mercy.

End of Decade: "Grace of the Resurrection come down into my soul and make me really faithful."[4]

Second Glorious Mystery: Ascension into Heaven

Petition: "We offer Thee, O Lord Jesus, this [...] decade in honor of Thy glorious Ascension, and we ask of Thee, through this mystery and through the intercession of Thy Blessed Mother, a firm hope and a great longing for Heaven."[5]

Setting: Now the eleven disciples went to Galilee, to the mountain to which Jesus had directed them. When they saw him, they worshiped him; but some doubted. (Mt 28:16-17, NRSV)

Our Father... And Jesus came and said to them, "All authority in heaven and on earth has been given to me. (Mt 28:18, NRSV)

Hail Mary... Go therefore and make disciples of all nations, baptizing them in the name of the Father and of the Son and of the Holy Spirit, (Mt 28:19, NRSV)

Hail Mary... and teaching them to obey everything that I have commanded you. And remember, I am with you always, to the end of the age." (Mt 28:20, NRSV)

Hail Mary... And he said to them, "Go into all the world and proclaim the good news to the whole creation. (Mk 16:15, NRSV)

Hail Mary... The one who believes and is baptized will be saved; but the one who does not believe will be condemned. (Mk 16:16, NRSV)

Hail Mary... And these signs will accompany those who believe: by using my name they will cast out demons; they will speak in new tongues; (Mk 16:17, NRSV)

The Ascension of the Lord / Giulio Campi / Chiesa di San Sigismondo, Cremona /
© Renata Sedmakova / Shutterstock.com

*Hail Mary...*Then he led them out as far as Bethany, and, lifting up his hands, he blessed them. (Lk 24:50, NRSV)

Hail Mary... But you will receive power when the Holy Spirit has come upon you; and you will be my witnesses in Jerusalem, in all

Judea and Samaria, and to the ends of the earth." (Acts 1:8, NRSV)

Hail Mary... When he had said this, as they were watching, he was lifted up, and a cloud took him out of their sight. (Acts 1:9, NRSV)

Hail Mary... While he was going and they were gazing up toward heaven, suddenly two men in white robes stood by them. (Acts 1:10, NRSV)

Hail Mary... They said, "Men of Galilee, why do you stand looking up toward heaven? This Jesus, who has been taken up from you into heaven, will come in the same way as you saw him go into heaven." (Acts 1:11, NRSV)

Glory Be... And they worshiped him, and returned to Jerusalem with great joy; (Lk 24:52, NRSV)

Fatima Prayer... O my Jesus, forgive us our sins, save us from the fires of hell, and lead all souls to Heaven, especially those in most need of Thy Mercy.

End of Decade: "Grace of the mystery of the Ascension of Our Lord, come down into my soul and make me ready for Heaven."[6]

Third Glorious Mystery: The Descent of the Holy Spirit

Petition: "We offer Thee, O Lord Jesus, this [...] decade in honor of thy mystery of Pentecost, and we ask of Thee, through this mystery and through the intercession of Mary, Thy most faithful Spouse, Thy holy wisdom so that we may know, really love and practice Thy truth, and make all others share in it."[7]

Setting: When the day of Pentecost had come, they were all together in one place. (Acts 2:1, NRSV)

Our Father... And suddenly from heaven there came a sound like the rush of a violent wind, and it filled the entire house where they were sitting. (Acts 2:2, NRSV)

The Descent of the Holy Ghost / Titian / Santa Maria della Salute, Venice, Italy /
© Renata Sedmakova / Shutterstock.com

Hail Mary... Divided tongues, as of fire, appeared among them, and a tongue rested on each of them. (Acts 2:3, NRSV)

Hail Mary... All of them were filled with the Holy Spirit and began to speak in other languages, as the Spirit gave them ability. (Acts 2:4, NRSV)

Hail Mary... Now there were devout Jews from every nation under heaven living in Jerusalem. And at this sound the crowd gathered and was bewildered, because each one heard them speaking in the native language of each. (Acts 2:5-6, NRSV)

Hail Mary... Amazed and astonished, they asked, "Are not all these who are speaking Galileans? And how is it that we hear, each of us, in our own native language? (Acts 2:7-8, NRSV)

Hail Mary... Parthians, Medes, Elamites, and residents of Mesopotamia, Judea and Cappadocia, Pontus and Asia, Phrygia and Pamphylia, Egypt and the parts of Libya belonging to Cyrene, (Acts 2:9-10a, NRSV)

Hail Mary... and visitors from Rome, both Jews and proselytes, Cretans and Arabs—in our own languages we hear them speaking about God's deeds of power." (Acts 2:10b-11, NRSV)

Hail Mary... All were amazed and perplexed, saying to one another, "What does this mean?" But others sneered and said, "They are filled with new wine." (Acts 2:12-13, NRSV)

Hail Mary... But Peter, standing with the eleven, raised his voice and addressed them, "Men of Judea and all who live in Jerusalem, let this be known to you, and listen to what I say. (Acts 2:14, NRSV)

Hail Mary... Indeed, these are not drunk, as you suppose, for it is only nine o'clock in the morning. No, this is what was spoken through the prophet Joel: (Acts 2:15-16, NRSV)

Hail Mary... 'In the last days it will be, God declares, that I will pour out my Spirit upon all flesh, and your sons and your daughters shall prophesy, (Acts 2:17a, NRSV)

Glory Be... Likewise the Spirit helps us in our weakness; for we do not know how to pray as we ought, but that very Spirit intercedes with sighs too deep for words. (Rom 8:26, NRSV)

Fatima Prayer... O my Jesus, forgive us our sins, save us from the fires of hell, and lead all souls to Heaven, especially those in most need of Thy Mercy.

End of Decade: "Grace of Pentecost, come down into my soul and make me really wise in the eyes of Almighty God."[8]

Fourth Glorious Mystery: The Assumption of Mary

Petition: "We offer Thee, O Lord Jesus, this [...] decade in honor of the Immaculate Conception and the Assumption of Thy holy and Blessed Mother, body and soul, into Heaven, and we ask of Thee, through these two mysteries and through her intercession, the gift of true devotion to her to help us live and die holily."[9]

Setting: But anyone united to the Lord becomes one spirit with him. (1 Cor 6:17, NRSV)

Our Father... So it is with the resurrection of the dead. What is sown is perishable, what is raised is imperishable. (1 Cor 15:42, NRSV)

Hail Mary... I will put enmity between you and the woman, and between your offspring and hers; he will strike your head, and you will strike his heel." (Gn 3:15, NRSV)

Hail Mary... Today is not the first time your wisdom has been shown, but from the beginning of your life all the people have recognized your understanding, for your heart's disposition is right. (Jdt 8:29, NRSV)

Hail Mary... Therefore my heart is glad, and my soul rejoices; my body also rests secure. (Ps 16:9, NRSV)

Assumption of Virgin Mary / Rubens / Cathedral of Our Lady, Antwerp, Belgium /
© Renata Sedmakova / Shutterstock.com

Hail Mary... Wisdom is radiant and unfading, and she is easily discerned by those who love her, and is found by those who seek her. (Wis 6:12, NRSV)

Hail Mary... He will transform the body of our humiliation that it may be conformed to the body of his glory, by the power that also enables him to make all things subject to himself. (Phil 3:21, NRSV)

Hail Mary... There is one glory of the sun, and another glory of the moon, and another glory of the stars; indeed, star differs from star in glory. (1 Cor 15:41, NRSV)

Hail Mary... And have them make me a sanctuary, so that I may dwell among them. (Ex 25:8a, NRSV)

Hail Mary... Behind the second curtain was a tent called the Holy of Holies. In it stood the golden altar of incense and the ark of the covenant overlaid on all sides with gold, in which there were a golden urn holding the manna, and Aaron's rod that budded, and the tablets of the covenant; (Heb 9:3-4, NRSV)

Hail Mary... By faith Enoch was taken so that he did not experience death; and "he was not found, because God had taken him." For it was attested before he was taken away that "he had pleased God." (Heb 11:5, NRSV)

Hail Mary... As they continued walking and talking, a chariot of fire and horses of fire separated the two of them, and Elijah ascended in a whirlwind into heaven. (2 Kgs 2:11, NRSV)

Glory Be... Then God's temple in heaven was opened, and the ark of his covenant was seen within his temple; (Rev 11:19a, NRSV)

Fatima Prayer... O my Jesus, forgive us our sins, save us from the fires of hell, and lead all souls to Heaven, especially those in most need of Thy Mercy.

End of Decade: "Grace of the Immaculate Conception and the Assumption of Mary, come down into my soul and make me truly devoted to her."[10]

Fifth Glorious Mystery: The Coronation of Mary

Petition: "We offer Thee, O Lord Jesus, this [...] decade in honor of the glorious crowning of Thy Blessed Mother in Heaven, and we ask of Thee, through this mystery and through Her intercession, the grace of perseverance and increase of virtue until the very moment of death and after that the eternal crown that is prepared for us. We ask the same grace of all the just and for all our benefactors."[11]

Setting: A great portent appeared in heaven: a woman clothed with the sun, with the moon under her feet, and on her head a crown of twelve stars. (Rev 12:1, NRSV)

Our Father... more than all the other women; of all the virgins she won his favor and devotion, so that he set the royal crown on her head and made her queen (Est 2:17b, NRSV)

Hail Mary... You shall be a crown of beauty in the hand of the LORD, and a royal diadem in the hand of your God. (Is 62:3, NRSV)

Hail Mary... then he sat on his throne, and had a throne brought for the king's mother, and she sat on his right. (1 Kgs 2:19b, NRSV)

Hail Mary... "Who is this that looks forth like the dawn, fair as the moon, bright as the sun, terrible as an army with banners?" (Sg 6:10, NRSV)

Hail Mary... When they met her, they all blessed her with one accord and said to her, "You are the glory of Jerusalem, you are the great boast of Israel, you are the great pride of our nation! (Jth 15:9, NRSV)

Hail Mary... Yet you have made them a little lower than God, and crowned them with glory and honor. (Ps 8:5, NRSV)

Coronation of Mother Mary by the Holy Trinity / Sanctuary of Fatima, Portugal / © jorisvo / Shutterstock.com

Hail Mary... Let us therefore approach the throne of grace with boldness, so that we may receive mercy and find grace to help in time of need. (Heb 4:16, NRSV)

Hail Mary... Humble yourselves before the Lord, and he will exalt you. (Jas 4:10, NRSV)

Hail Mary... Therefore they will receive a glorious crown and a beautiful diadem from the hand of the Lord, because with his right hand he will cover them, and with his arm he will shield them. (Wis 5:16, NRSV)

Hail Mary... He has brought down the powerful from their thrones, and lifted up the lowly; (Lk 1:52, NRSV)

Hail Mary... Blessed is anyone who endures temptation. Such a one has stood the test and will receive the crown of life that the Lord has promised to those who love him. (Jas 1:12, NRSV)

Glory Be... You are altogether beautiful, my love; there is no flaw in you. (Sg 4:7, NRSV)

Fatima Prayer... O my Jesus, forgive us our sins, save us from the fires of hell, and lead all souls to Heaven, especially those in most need of Thy Mercy.

End of Decade: "Grace of the Coronation of Mary, come down into my soul and help me to resist temptation and receive the eternal crown of life."[12]

Hail, Holy Queen... Hail, holy Queen, Mother of mercy, our life, our sweetness and our hope. To thee do we cry, poor banished children of Eve. To thee do we send up our sighs, mourning and weeping in this valley of tears. Turn then, most gracious Advocate, thine eyes of mercy toward us, and after this our exile, show unto us the blessed fruit of thy womb, Jesus. O clement, O loving, O sweet Virgin Mary. Pray for us, O Holy Mother of God. That we may be made worthy of the promises of Christ. Amen.

Concluding Prayer... "We beseech Thee, dear Lord Jesus by the [...] mysteries of Thy life, passion and death, by Thy glory and by the merits of Thy Blessed Mother, to convert sinners and help the dying, to deliver the Holy Souls from Purgatory and to give us all Thy grace so that we may live well and die well—and please give us the Light of Thy Glory later on so that we may see Thee face to face and love Thee for all eternity. Amen. So be it."[13]

CHAPTER 9

LUMINOUS MYSTERIES

St. John Paul II suggested praying the Luminous Mysteries on Thursday. The five Luminous Mysteries are:
- The Baptism of Jesus
- First Miracle at the Wedding Feast of Cana
- Proclamation of the Kingdom of God
- The Transfiguration
- The Institution of the Eucharist

Introductory Prayers

Sign of the Cross...

Prayer of Unity: "I unite myself with all the Saints in Heaven, and with all the just on earth; I unite myself with Thee, my Jesus, in order to praise Thy Holy Mother worthily and to praise Thee in her and by her. I renounce all the distractions that may come to me while I am saying this Rosary which I wish to say with modesty, attention, and devotion, just as if it were to be the last of my life."[1]

Petition: "We offer Thee, O most Holy Trinity, this Creed in honor of all the mysteries of our faith, this Our Father and these three Hail Marys in honor of the unity of Thy Essence and the Trinity of Thy Persons. We ask of Thee a lively faith, a firm hope and an ardent charity. Amen."[2]

Apostles' Creed... My soul thirsts for God, for the living God. When shall I come and behold the face of God? (Ps 42:2, NRSV)

Our Father... he has sent me to bring good news to the oppressed, to bind up the brokenhearted, to proclaim liberty to the captives, and release to the prisoners; (Is 61:1b, NRSV)

Hail Mary... Those who eat my flesh and drink my blood have eternal life, and I will raise them up on the last day; (Jn 6:54, NRSV)

Hail Mary... I will lead the blind by a road they do not know, by paths they have not known I will guide them. (Is 42:16a, NRSV)

Hail Mary... I will turn the darkness before them into light, the rough places into level ground. These are the things I will do, and I will not forsake them. (Is 42:16b, NRSV)

Glory Be... Blessed are those who have not seen and yet have come to believe." (Jn 20:29b, NRSV)

First Luminous Mystery: The Baptism of Jesus

Petition: We offer Thee, O Lord Jesus, this decade in honor of Thy Baptism, and we ask of Thee, through this mystery and through the intercession of Thy Blessed Mother, to enkindle in our hearts a deep gratitude for Thy perfect identification with us, sinners as we are, and the grace to recognize and repent of our own sinfulness.[3]

Setting: In those days John the Baptist appeared in the wilderness of Judea, proclaiming, "Repent, for the kingdom of heaven has come near." (Mt 3:1-2, NRSV)

Our Father... This is the one of whom the prophet Isaiah spoke when he said, "The voice of one crying out in the wilderness: 'Prepare the way of the Lord, make his paths straight.'" (Mt 3:3, NRSV)

The Baptism of Christ / Juan Fernandez de Navarrete / Museo Nacional del Prado, Madrid, Spain / Art Resource, NY

Hail Mary... John the baptizer appeared in the wilderness, proclaiming a baptism of repentance for the forgiveness of sins. (Mk 1:4, NRSV)

Hail Mary... And people from the whole Judean countryside and all the people of Jerusalem were going out to him, and were baptized by him in the river Jordan, confessing their sins. (Mk 1:5, NRSV)

Hail Mary... Now John was clothed with camel's hair, with a leather belt around his waist, and he ate locusts and wild honey. (Mk 1:6, NRSV)

Hail Mary... He proclaimed, "The one who is more powerful than I is coming after me; I am not worthy to stoop down and untie the thong of his sandals. (Mk 1:7, NRSV)

Hail Mary... I have baptized you with water; but he will baptize you with the Holy Spirit." (Mk 1:8, NRSV)

Hail Mary... Then Jesus came from Galilee to John at the Jordan, to be baptized by him. (Mt 3:13, NRSV)

Hail Mary... John would have prevented him, saying, "I need to be baptized by you, and do you come to me?" (Mt 3:14, NRSV)

Hail Mary... But Jesus answered him, "Let it be so now; for it is proper for us in this way to fulfill all righteousness." Then he consented. (Mt 3:15, NRSV)

Hail Mary... And just as he was coming up out of the water, he saw the heavens torn apart and the Spirit descending like a dove on him. (Mk 1:10, NRSV)

Hail Mary... And a voice came from heaven, "You are my Son, the Beloved; with you I am well pleased." (Mk 1:11, NRSV)

Glory Be... And baptism, which this prefigured, now saves you—not as a removal of dirt from the body, but as an appeal to God for a good conscience, through the resurrection of Jesus Christ, (1 Pt 3:21, NRSV)

Fatima Prayer... O my Jesus, forgive us our sins, save us from the fires of hell, and lead all souls to Heaven, especially those in most need of Thy Mercy.

End of Decade: Grace of the mystery of Our Lord's Baptism, come down into my soul to help me recognize my own sinfulness and to fully repent.

Second Luminous Mystery: First Miracle at the Wedding Feast of Cana

Petition: We offer Thee, O Lord Jesus, this decade in honor of Thy First Miracle at the Wedding Feast of Cana, and we ask of Thee, through this mystery and through the intercession of Thy Blessed Mother, for the grace to respond to the requests of others with a spirit of self-sacrifice.

Setting: On the third day there was a wedding in Cana in Galilee, and the mother of Jesus was there. (Jn 2:1, NRSV)

Our Father... Jesus and his disciples had also been invited to the wedding. (Jn 2:2, NRSV)

Hail Mary... When the wine gave out, the mother of Jesus said to him, "They have no wine." (Jn 2:3, NRSV)

Hail Mary... And Jesus said to her, "Woman, what concern is that to you and to me? My hour has not yet come." (Jn 2:4, NRSV)

Hail Mary... His mother said to the servants, "Do whatever he tells you." (Jn 2:5, NRSV)

Hail Mary... Now standing there were six stone water jars for the Jewish rites of purification, each holding twenty or thirty gallons. (Jn 2:6, NRSV)

Hail Mary... Jesus said to them, "Fill the jars with water." And they filled them up to the brim. (Jn 2:7, NRSV)

Hail Mary... He said to them, "Now draw some out, and take it to the chief steward." So they took it. (Jn 2:8, NRSV)

Hail Mary... When the steward tasted the water that had become wine, and did not know where it came from (though the servants who had drawn the water knew), the steward called the bridegroom (Jn 2:9, NRSV)

Miracle at Cana / Maerten de Voos / Cathedral of Our Lady, Antwerp, Belgium / © Renata Sedmakova / Shutterstock.com

Hail Mary... and said to him, "Everyone serves the good wine first, and then the inferior wine after the guests have become drunk. But you have kept the good wine until now." (Jn 2:10, NRSV)

Hail Mary... Jesus did this, the first of his signs, in Cana of Galilee, and revealed his glory; and his disciples believed in him. (Jn 2:11, NRSV)

Hail Mary... Let us rejoice and exult and give him the glory, for the marriage of the Lamb has come, and his bride has made herself ready; (Rev 19:7, NRSV)

Glory Be... We will exult and rejoice in you; we will extol your love more than wine; rightly do they love you. (Sg 1:4b, NRSV)

Fatima Prayer... O my Jesus, forgive us our sins, save us from the fires of hell, and lead all souls to Heaven, especially those in most need of Thy Mercy.

End of Decade: Grace of the mystery of Thy First Miracle at the Wedding Feast of Cana, come down into my soul and increase my sacrificial love for others so as to deepen the expression of my love for Thee, my Eternal Bridegroom.

Third Luminous Mystery: Proclamation of the Kingdom of God

Petition: We offer Thee, O Lord Jesus, this decade in honor of Thy Proclamation of the Kingdom of God, and we ask of Thee, through this mystery and through the intercession of Thy Blessed Mother, for the courage and discernment to share our faith with those who do not know Thee.

Setting: Now after John was arrested, Jesus came to Galilee, proclaiming the good news of God, and saying, "The time is fulfilled, and the kingdom of God has come near; repent, and believe in the good news." (Mk 1:14-15, NRSV)

Our Father... "The kingdom of God is not coming with things that can be observed; nor will they say, 'Look, here it is!' or 'There it is!' For, in fact, the kingdom of God is among you." (Lk 17:20b-21, NRSV)

Hail Mary... As you go, proclaim the good news, 'The kingdom of heaven has come near.' Cure the sick, raise the dead, cleanse the lepers, cast out demons. (Mt 10:7-8a, NRSV)

Hail Mary... Soon afterwards he went on through cities and villages, proclaiming and bringing the good news of the kingdom of God. The twelve were with him, (Lk 8:1, NRSV)

Hail Mary... When Jesus saw the crowds, he went up the mountain; and after he sat down, his disciples came to him. Then he began to speak, and taught them, saying: "Blessed are the poor in spirit, for theirs is the kingdom of heaven. (Mt 5:1-3, NRSV)

Hail Mary... "Blessed are those who are persecuted for righteousness' sake, for theirs is the kingdom of heaven. (Mt 5:10, NRSV)

Hail Mary... Truly I tell you, whoever does not receive the kingdom of God as a little child will never enter it." (Mk 10:15, NRSV)

Hail Mary... "Not everyone who says to me, 'Lord, Lord,' will enter the kingdom of heaven, but only the one who does the will of my Father in heaven." (Mt 7:21, NRSV)

Hail Mary... Then Jesus looked around and said to his disciples, "How hard it will be for those who have wealth to enter the kingdom of God!" (Mk 10:23, NRSV)

Hail Mary... And the disciples were perplexed at these words. But Jesus said to them again, "Children, how hard it is to enter the kingdom of God!" (Mk 10:24, NRSV)

Hail Mary... For the kingdom of God is not food and drink but righteousness and peace and joy in the Holy Spirit. (Rom 14:17, NRSV)

Hail Mary... Jesus answered, "Very truly, I tell you, no one can enter the kingdom of God without being born of water and Spirit. (Jn 3:5, NRSV)

Glory Be... After his suffering he presented himself alive to them by many convincing proofs, appearing to them during forty days and speaking about the kingdom of God. (Acts 1:3)

Christ Healing the Sick / James Tissot / HIP / Art Resource, NY

Fatima Prayer... O my Jesus, forgive us our sins, save us from the fires of hell, and lead all souls to Heaven, especially those in most need of Thy Mercy.

End of Decade: Grace of the mystery of Thy Proclamation of the Kingdom of God come into my soul and help me discern the best way to courageously share my faith with those who do not know Thee.

Fourth Luminous Mystery: The Transfiguration

Petition: We offer Thee, O Lord Jesus, this decade in honor of Thy Transfiguration and we ask of Thee, through this mystery and through the intercession of Thy Blessed Mother, for the grace to be conformed into Thy likeness by which our nature is united to Thee.

Setting: Six days later, Jesus took with him Peter and James and his brother John and led them up a high mountain, by themselves. (Mt 17:1, NRSV)

Our Father... And he was transfigured before them, and his face shone like the sun, and his clothes became dazzling white. (Mt 17:2, NRSV)

Hail Mary... Suddenly they saw two men, Moses and Elijah, talking to him. They appeared in glory and were speaking of his departure, which he was about to accomplish at Jerusalem. (Lk 9:30-31, NRSV)

Hail Mary... Now Peter and his companions were weighed down with sleep; but since they had stayed awake, they saw his glory and the two men who stood with him. (Lk 9:32, NRSV)

Hail Mary... Then Peter said to Jesus, "Lord, it is good for us to be here; (Mt 17:4a, NRSV)

Transfiguration / Pietro Perugino / Collegio del Cambio, Perugia, Italy / Scala /
Art Resource, NY

Hail Mary... if you wish, I will make three dwellings here, one for you, one for Moses, and one for Elijah." (Mt 17:4b, NRSV)

Hail Mary... While he was still speaking, suddenly a bright cloud overshadowed them, and from the cloud a voice said, "This is my

Son, the Beloved; with him I am well pleased; listen to him!" (Mt 17:5, NRSV)

Hail Mary... When the disciples heard this, they fell to the ground and were overcome by fear. (Mt 17:6, NRSV)

Hail Mary... But Jesus came and touched them, saying, "Get up and do not be afraid." (Mt 17:7, NRSV)

Hail Mary... And when they looked up, they saw no one except Jesus himself alone. (Mt 17:8, NRSV)

Hail Mary... As they were coming down the mountain, Jesus ordered them, "Tell no one about the vision until after the Son of Man has been raised from the dead." (Mt 17:9, NRSV)

Hail Mary... For he received honor and glory from God the Father when that voice was conveyed to him by the Majestic Glory, saying, "This is my Son, my Beloved, with whom I am well pleased." (2 Pt 1:17, NRSV)

*Glory Be...*We ourselves heard this voice come from heaven, while we were with him on the holy mountain. (2 Pt 1:18, NRSV)

Fatima Prayer... O my Jesus, forgive us our sins, save us from the fires of hell, and lead all souls to Heaven, especially those in most need of Thy Mercy.

End of Decade: Grace of the mystery of Thy Transfiguration come into my soul and form me into Thy likeness increasingly each day.

Fifth Luminous Mystery: The Institution of the Eucharist

Petition: We offer Thee, O Lord Jesus, this decade in honor of Thy Institution of the Eucharist, and we ask of Thee, through this mystery and through the intercession of Thy Blessed Mother, for an insatiable hunger and thirst for Thy Body and Thy Blood.

Setting: Then came the day of Unleavened Bread, on which the Passover lamb had to be sacrificed. So Jesus sent Peter and John, saying, "Go and prepare the Passover meal for us that we may eat it." They asked him, "Where do you want us to make preparations for it?" (Lk 22:7-9, NRSV)

Our Father... "Listen," he said to them, "when you have entered the city, a man carrying a jar of water will meet you; follow him into the house he enters (Lk 22:10, NRSV)

Hail Mary... So they went and found everything as he had told them; and they prepared the Passover meal. (Lk 22:13, NRSV)

Hail Mary... When the hour came, he took his place at the table, and the apostles with him. (Lk 22:14, NRSV)

Hail Mary... He said to them, "I have eagerly desired to eat this Passover with you before I suffer; (Lk 22:15, NRSV)

Hail Mary... for I tell you, I will not eat it until it is fulfilled in the kingdom of God." (Lk 22:16, NRSV)

Hail Mary... Then he took a cup, and after giving thanks he said, "Take this and divide it among yourselves; (Lk 22:17, NRSV)

Hail Mary... for I tell you that from now on I will not drink of the fruit of the vine until the kingdom of God comes." (Lk 22:18, NRSV)

Hail Mary... Then he took a loaf of bread, and when he had given thanks, he broke it and gave it to them, saying, "This is my body, which is given for you. Do this in remembrance of me." (Lk 22:19, NRSV)

Hail Mary... And he did the same with the cup after supper, saying, "This cup that is poured out for you is the new covenant in my blood. (Lk 22:20, NRSV)

The Last Supper / Juan de Juanes / Museo Nacional del Prado, Madrid, Spain / Art Resource, NY

Hail Mary... I am the living bread that came down from heaven. Whoever eats of this bread will live forever; and the bread that I will give for the life of the world is my flesh." (Jn 6:51, NRSV)

Hail Mary... The cup of blessing that we bless, is it not a sharing in the blood of Christ? The bread that we break, is it not a sharing in the body of Christ? (1 Cor 10:16, NRSV)

Glory Be... Those who eat my flesh and drink my blood abide in me, and I in them. (Jn 6:56, NRSV)

Fatima Prayer... O my Jesus, forgive us our sins, save us from the fires of hell, and lead all souls to Heaven, especially those in most need of Thy Mercy.

End of Decade: Grace of the mystery of Thy Institution of the Eucharist come into my soul and draw me to Thy precious Body and Blood for spiritual nourishment.

Hail, Holy Queen... Hail, holy Queen, Mother of mercy, our life, our sweetness and our hope. To thee do we cry, poor banished children of Eve. To thee do we send up our sighs, mourning and weeping in this valley of tears. Turn then, most gracious Advocate, thine eyes of mercy toward us, and after this our exile, show unto us the blessed fruit of thy womb, Jesus. O clement, O loving, O sweet Virgin Mary. Pray for us, O Holy Mother of God. That we may be made worthy of the promises of Christ. Amen.

Concluding Prayer... "We beseech Thee, dear Lord Jesus by the [...] mysteries of Thy life, passion and death, by Thy glory and by the merits of Thy Blessed Mother, to convert sinners and help the dying, to deliver the Holy Souls from Purgatory and to give us all Thy grace so that we may live well and die well—and please give us the Light of Thy Glory later on so that we may see Thee face to face and love Thee for all eternity. Amen. So be it."[4]

Bead by Bead: The Scriptural Rosary

CHAPTER 10

PRAYER TO THE TRINITY

*The Holy Trinity / Unknown artist of 19th century / The Church of the Holy Sepulchre /
Jerusalem, Israel / © Renata Sedmakova / Shutterstock.com*

O my God, Trinity whom I adore, help me forget myself entirely so to establish myself in you, unmovable and peaceful as if my soul were already in eternity. May nothing be able to trouble my peace or make me leave you, O my unchanging God, but may each minute bring me more deeply into your mystery! Grant my soul peace. Make it your heaven, your beloved dwelling and the place of your rest. May I never abandon you there, but may I be there, whole and entire, completely vigilant in my faith, entirely adoring, and wholly given over to your creative action.[1]

~ Prayer of Blessed Sr. Elizabeth of the Trinity

My Immaculate Heart will be your refuge, and the way that will lead you to God.[2]

~ Our Lady of Fatima to Lucia, June 13, 1917

APPENDIX

This Appendix contains references that are a reasonable starting place for those wishing to dig deeper into a variety of topics in their faith journey. I found these resources to be especially encouraging, educational, and inspirational. Many were also helpful to my husband, who holds a Masters of Divinity from a prestigious Protestant seminary and spent his early post-graduate career as a Protestant pastor. He entered the Catholic Church in 2013.

TOPIC: Rosary
- Donald H. Calloway, MIC, *Champions of the Rosary*, (Stockbridge, MA: Marian Press, 2016).
- Saint Louis Mary de Montfort, *The Secret of the Rosary*, trans. Mary Barbour, T.O.P. (Charlotte, NC: Saint Benedict Press,TAN Books, 1987).
- John D. Miller, *Beads and Prayers: The Rosary in History and Devotion*, (London, UK: Burns & Oates, 2002).

TOPIC: Mariology
- Saint Louis Mary de Montfort, *True Devotion to Mary*, trans. Father Frederick William Faber, D.D. (Charlotte, NC: Saint Benedict Press,TAN Books, 2010).
- Fulton J. Sheen, *The World's First Love*, (San Francisco, CA: Ignatius Press, 2011).

- Scott Hahn, *Hail, Holy Queen: The Mother of God in the Word of God,* (New York, NY: Doubleday, 2001).
- Killian J. Healy, O.Carm, *The Assumption of Mary,* (Darien, IL: Carmelite Media, 2011).
- Edward P. Sri, *Queen Mother: A Biblical Theology of Mary's Queenship,* (Steubenville, OH: Emmaus Road Publishing, 2005).

TOPIC: Personal Spiritual Growth, HAPP

- Michael E. Gaitley, MIC, *33 Days to Morning Glory : A Do-It-Yourself Retreat In Preparation for Marian Consecration,* (Stockbridge, MA: Marian Press, 2013).
- Michael E. Gaitley, MIC, *Consoling the Heart of Jesus: A Do-It-Yourself Retreat—Inspired by the Spiritual Exercises of St. Ignatius,* (Stockbridge, MA: Marian Press, 2010).
- Michael E. Gaitley, MIC, *The One Thing Is Three: How the Most Holy Trinity Explains Everything,* (Stockbridge, MA: Marian Press, 2012).
- Ralph Martin, *The Fulfillment of All Desire,* (Steubenville, OH: Emmaus Road Publishing, 2006).
- Fr. Reginald Garrigou-Lagrange, O.P., *Knowing the Love of God: Lessons from a Spiritual Master,* (Dekalb, IL: Lighthouse Catholic Media, 2016).

TOPIC: Early Church Fathers

- Mike Aquilina, *The Fathers of the Church.* 3rd ed., (Huntington, IN: Our Sunday Visitor Publishing Division, 2013).
- Pope Benedict XVI, *Church Fathers: From Clement of Rome to Augustine,* (San Francisco, CA: Ignatius Press, 2008).
- Rod Bennett, *Four Witnesses: The Early Church in Her Own Words,* (San Francisco, CA: Ignatius Press, 2012).

TOPIC: Catholic Apologetics

- Dave Armstrong, *Bible Proofs for Catholic Truths,* (Manchester, NH: Sophia Institute Press, 2009).
- G.K. Chesterton, *Common Sense 101,* (San Francisco, CA: Ignatius Press, 2006).
- G.K. Chesterton, *The Everlasting Man,* (Nashville, TN: Sam Torode Book Arts, 2014).

- Basil Christopher Butler, *Always Inspired: Why Bible-Believing Christians Need the Catholic Church*, (Manchester, NH: Sophia Press, 2012).

TOPIC: Seekers, Converts, and Reverts

- David Currie, *Born Fundamentalist, Born Again Catholic*, (San Francisco, CA: Ignatius Press, 1996).
- Jennifer Fulwiler, *Something Other Than God: How I Passionately Sought Happiness and Accidentally Found It*, (San Francisco, CA: Ignatius Press, 2014).
- Scott and Kimberly Hahn, *Rome Sweet Home: Our Journey to Catholicism*, (San Francisco, CA: Ignatius Press, 1993).
- Alex Jones, *No Price too High: A Pentecostal Preacher Becomes Catholic.* (San Francisco, CA: Ignatius Press, 2006).
- Mathew Kelly, *Rediscover Catholicism*, 2nd ed. (North Palm Beach, FL: Beacon Publishing, 2010).
- Stephen K. Ray, *Crossing the Tiber*, (San Francisco, CA: Ignatius Press, 1997).

TOPIC: Digging Deeper into Catholic Theology

- *Catechism of the Catholic Church.* 2nd ed. Vatican: Libreria Editrice Vaticana, 2000. Print.
- Scott Hahn, *The Lamb's Supper: The Mass as Heaven on Earth*, (New York, NY: Image, 1999).
- Brant Pitre, *Jesus and the Jewish Roots of the Eucharist: Unlocking the Secrets of the Last Supper*, (New York, NY: Doubleday, 2011).
- Brandt Pitre, *Jesus the Bridegroom: The Greatest Love Story Ever Told*, (New York, NY: Image, 2014).
- Frank Sheed, *Theology and Sanity*, (San Francisco, CA: Ignatius Press, 1993).

TOPIC: Writings of the Saints and Blesseds

- Saint Augustine, *Confessions*, trans. Henry Chadwick. (Oxford, England: Oxford University Press, 2008).
- (Blessed) Angela of Foligna, *Angela of Foligno: Complete Works (Classics of Western Spirituality)*, trans. Paul LaChance, O.F.M. (New York, NY: Paulist Press, 1993).

- St. Catherine of Siena, *The Dialogue of St. Catherine of Siena*, trans. Algar Throrold. (Mineolan, NY: Dover Publications, 2007).
- St. Francis de Sales, *Introduction to the Devout Life*, (San Francisco and Greenwood Village, CO: Ignatius Press-Augustine Institute, 2015).
- St. John of the Cross, *The Collected Works of St. John of the Cross* Revised Edition, trans. Kieran Kavanaugh, O.C.D. and Otilio Rodríquez, O.C.D. (Washington, DC: ICS Publications, 1991).
- St. Maria Faustina Kowalska, *Diary: Divine Mercy in My Soul*, trans. Marians of the Immaculate Conception. (Stockbridge, MA: Marian Press, 2011).
- St. Teresa of Ávila, *Interior Castle,* trans. E. Allison Peers. (London, UK: Penguin Books, 1957).
- St. Teresa of Ávila, *The Life of Saint Teresa of Ávila by Herself*, trans. J. M. Cohen. (London, UK: Penguin Books, 1957).
- St. Thérèse of Lisieux, *Story of a Soul*, trans. John Clark, O.C.D. (Washington, DC: ICS Publications, 1996).

TOPIC: Lectio Divina
- Tim Gray, *Praying Scripture for a Change: An Introduction to Lectio Divina*, (West Chester, PA: Ascension Press, 2009).
- Tim Gray, *Prayer: Finding Intimacy with God*, Lectio Series, (Greenwood Village, CO: Augustine Institute, 2016).

TOPIC: Catholic Views on Sexuality (Theology of the Body)
- Mary Healy, *Men and Women Are From Eden: A Study Guide to John Paul II's Theology of the Body*, (Cincinnati, OH: Servant Books, 2005).
- Christopher West, *Theology of the Body for Beginners: A Basic Introduction to Pope John Paul II's Sexual Revolution*, (West Chester, PA: Ascension Press, 2009).

TOPIC: End Times
- David B. Currie, *Rapture: The End-Times Error That Leaves the Bible Behind*, (Manchester, NH: Sophia Press, 2003).
- Scott Hahn, *The End: A Study on the Book of Revelation*, (Sycamore, IL: St. Joseph Communications, 2003).

TOPIC: Approved Translations of the Entire Bible

- New American Bible, Revised Edition (NABRE).
- New Revised Standard Version, Catholic Edition, National Council of Churches (NRSV-CE).
- For more information see, http://usccb.org/bible/approved-translations.

TOPIC: Digital Resources

FORMED (https://formed.org) is an online platform produced by the Augustine Institute in Greenwood Village, CO. It features hundreds of Catholic videos, audio talks, eBooks and movies from many well-respected Catholic apostolates.

Bead by Bead: The Scriptural Rosary

ENDNOTES

DEDICATION

[1] For the exact statements that Bernardo Martinez made to Bishop, Mons. Pablo Antonio Vega Mantilla, Roman Catholic Bishop of Juigalpa, Nicaragua, see Google shortened URL: https://goo.gl/xnEXM5. Accessed on February 23, 2017. The excerpt [Donald H. Calloway, MIC, *Champions of the Rosary*, (Stockbridge, MA: Marian Press, 2016), p. 148] is a summary of a conversation between the Virgin Mary and Martinez as told to the Bishop.

IN GRATITUDE

[1] The *Scriptural Rosary: The Sorrowful Mysteries* may be found on the United States Conference of Catholic Bishops website. See Google shortened URL: https://goo.gl/WzUWUt. Accessed online February 23, 2017.

[2] Michael E. Gaitley, MIC, *33 Days to Morning Glory: A Do-It-Yourself Retreat In Preparation for Marian Consecration*, (Stockbridge, MA: Marian Press, 2013).

[3] The Hearts Afire: Parish-based Programs (HAPP) from the Marian Fathers of the Immaculate Conception was officially released on Divine Mercy Sunday, April 15, 2012. For an overview, see Google shortened URL: https://goo.gl/hoOEoL. Accessed on February 23, 2017.

[4] Donald H. Calloway, MIC, *Champions of the Rosary*, (Stockbridge, MA: Marian Press, 2016).

INTRODUCTION

[1] Fulton J. Sheen, *The World's First Love*, (San Francisco, CA: Ignatius Press, 2011), p. 215.
[2] St. Louis Mary de Montfort, *The Secret of the Rosary*, trans. Mary Barbour, T.O.P. (Charlotte, NC: Saint Benedict Press, TAN Books, 1987).

THE SOIL: SHORT HISTORY OF THE ROSARY

[1] Donald H. Calloway, MIC, *Champions of the Rosary*, (Stockbridge, MA: Marian Press, 2016), p. 26.
[2] The breviary is a book that contains the official set of daily prayers, psalms, hymns, and readings for particular hours each day, taking into account the liturgical season. The breviary is often used synonymously with the Divine Office or Liturgy of the Hours. For more information see, https://divineoffice.org.
[3] For more information on indulgences and the treasury of the Saints, see *Catechism of the Catholic Church*. 2nd ed. Vatican: Libreria Editrice Vaticana, 2000. Print. In-text citation: (Catholic Church 1471 - 1479).
[4] An apostolic constitution or letter, such as *Munificentissimus Deus* (1950), is a solemn pronouncement on matters of faith, whereas an encyclical is broader in scope and more pastoral in nature.
[5] Dom Augustine Marie, OSB, *The Message of Our Lady of Fatima (Selections)*, Google shortened URL: https://goo.gl/biem9Q, pg. 1. Accessed online February 23, 2017.
[6] Ibid, pg. 5.
[7] Apostolic Exhortation of his Holiness Paul VI, *Marialis Cultus*, w2.vatican.va/content/paul-vi/... Website for apostolic exhortations in English, see Google shortened URL: https://goo.gl/ockhHi. Accessed online February 23, 2017.
[8] Apostolic Letter of his Holiness John Paul II, *Rosarium Virginis Mariae*, w2.vatican.va/content/john-paul-ii/... Website for apostolic letters in English, see Google shortened URL: https://goo.gl/sPNqhq. Accessed online February 23, 2017, section 1.

[9] Ibid, section 4.
[10] St. Louis Mary de Montfort, *The Secret of the Rosary*, pg. 128.

THE SEEDS: FORMAT AND BASIC PRAYERS

[1] St. Louis Mary de Montfort, *The Secret of the Rosary*, pg. 11.
[2] St. Louis Mary de Montfort, *True Devotion to Mary*, pg. 293.
[3] St. Louis Mary de Montfort, *The Secret of the Rosary*, pp. 132-133.

THE FERTILIZER: ESSENTIAL NUTRIENTS

[1] G.K. Chesterton, *The Everlasting Man*, (Nashville, TN: Sam Torode Book Arts, 2014), pg 274 e-text.
[2] Fr. Michael Gaitley, MIC, *Vatican II, Mercy, and You*, Lighthouse Talk, (Greenwood Village, CO: Augustine Institute, 2016), contained within track 8.
[3] CARA Survey from 2008, Georgetown University, http://cara.georgetown.edu/sacraments.html. Accessed online on February 23, 2017. To understand what Catholics believe about the Real Presence of Christ in the Eucharist, see Google shortened URL: https://goo.gl/VLJiyV. Accessed online from the usccb.org website, February 23, 2017.
[4] Sherry A. Weddell, *Forming Intentional Disciples*, (Huntington, IN: Our Sunday Visitor Publishing Division, 2012).
[5] Pew Research Center, May 12, 2015, "America's Changing Religious Landscape." Google shortened URL: https://goo.gl/QVx9gD, pg 9. Accessed online on February 23, 2017.
[6] Ibid, pg 6.
[7] FORMED is a digital platform created and licensed by the Augustine Institute in Greenwood Village, Colorado. General information regarding FORMED may be viewed at https://formed.org. Accessed February 23, 2017.
[8] Apostolic Constitution of his Holiness Pius XII, *Munificentissimus Deus*, w2.vatican.va/content/pius-xii/... Website for apostolic constitutions in English. Google shortened URL: https://goo.gl/UAU7UX, sections 3-6. Accessed online February 23, 2017.
[9] Ibid, section 45.
[10] Tim Gray, *Praying Scripture for a Change: An Introduction to Lectio Divina*, (West Chester, PA: Ascension Press, 2009).

[11] Tim Gray, *Prayer: Finding Intimacy with God*, Lectio Series Study Guide, (Greenwood Village, CO: Augustine Institute, 2016), pg. 2.

[12] Tim Gray, *Praying Scripture for a Change: An Introduction to Lectio Divina*. See chapters 1 and 2.

[13] Apostolic Letter of his Holiness John Paul II, *Rosarium Virginis Mariae*, section 29.

[14] Ibid, section 30.

THE HARVEST: MY JOURNEY TO THE ROSARY

[1] St. Louis Mary de Montfort, *The Secret of the Rosary*, pg. 137.

[2] The New Living Translation (NLT) is one of the several Bible translations that I was using at the time. The NLT is a widely used translation in the Protestant community. The NRSV-Catholic Edition of Matthew (6:7) reads, "When you are praying, do not heap up empty phrases as the Gentiles do; for they think that they will be heard because of their many words. Do not heap up empty phrases." The prayers of the Rosary are hardly empty phrases, given their biblical roots!

[3] Apostolic Exhortation of his Holiness Paul VI, *Marialis Cultus*, section 45.

[4] Michael E. Gaitley, MIC, *33 Days to Morning Glory: A Do-It-Yourself Retreat In Preparation for Marian Consecration*, (Stockbridge, MA: Marian Press, 2013).

[5] In 1966, and reaffirmed in 1983, the U.S. Conference of Bishops issued the "Pastoral Statement on Penance and Abstinence," which allowed U.S. Catholics to eat meat on Fridays outside Lent provided another kind of penance was substituted. Google shortened URL: https://goo.gl/r2ixHl. Accessed on February 23, 2017.

[6] At the time that the author facilitated the HAPP program in her home parish, there were three parts: *33 Days to Morning Glory*, *Consoling the Heart of Jesus*, and *Wisdom and Works of Mercy*. Since then, the Marian Fathers have expanded the program. See https://www.allheartsafire.org/. Accessed online February 23, 2017.

[7] As I understand Fr. Gaitley's working definition, "God-events" are events that Christ participated in "after" the Incarnation. Since Christ is fully human and fully divine, His actions have the unique attribute of occurring both in human time and outside of time (in eternity). This idea is presented multiple times in the

HAPP *Consoling the Heart of Jesus* video lectures that are part of the HAPP DVD program. St. Josemaría Escrivá proposed a similar concept where time blends with eternity in the Mass. See Josemariá Escrivá, *Christ is Passing By*, (New York, NY: ScepterPublishers, 1974), pg. 142.

[8] *Catechism of the Catholic Church.* 2nd ed. Vatican: Libreria Editrice Vaticana, 2000. Print. In-text citation: (Catholic Church 234).

[9] The first time I ever heard that phrase was in the book by Fr. Michael E. Gaitley, MIC, *Consoling the Heart of Jesus: A Do-It-Yourself Retreat—Inspired by the Spiritual Exercises of St. Ignatius*, (Stockbridge, MA: Marian Press, 2010).

[10] Donald H. Calloway, MIC, *Champions of the Rosary*, (Stockbridge, MA: Marian Press, 2016), pp. 36-38.

[11] The *Scriptural Rosary: The Sorrowful Mysteries* may be found on the United States Conference of Catholic Bishops website, Google shortened URL: https://goo.gl/WzUWUt. Accessed online February 23, 2017.

JOYFUL MYSTERIES

[1] St. Louis Mary de Montfort, *True Devotion to Mary*, pg. 293.
[2] Ibid.
[3] St. Louis Mary de Montfort, *The Secret of the Rosary*, pg. 129.
[4] Ibid.
[5] Ibid.
[6] Ibid.
[7] Ibid.
[8] Ibid.
[9] Ibid.
[10] Ibid, pg. 130.
[11] Ibid.
[12] Ibid.
[13] Ibid, pp. 132-133.

SORROWFUL MYSTERIES

[1] St. Louis Mary de Montfort, *True Devotion to Mary*, pg. 293.
[2] Ibid.
[3] St. Louis Mary de Montfort, *The Secret of the Rosary*, pg. 129.
[4] Ibid, pg. 130.
[5] Ibid.

6 Ibid.
7 Ibid, pp. 130-131.
8 Ibid, pg. 131.
9 Ibid.
10 Ibid.
11 Ibid.
12 Ibid.
13 Ibid, pp. 132-133.

GLORIOUS MYSTERIES

1 St. Louis Mary de Montfort, *True Devotion to Mary*, pg. 293.
2 Ibid.
3 St. Louis Mary de Montfort, *The Secret of the Rosary*, pg. 131.
4 Ibid.
5 Ibid, pp. 131-132.
6 Ibid, pg. 132.
7 Ibid.
8 Ibid.
9 Ibid.
10 Ibid.
11 Ibid.
12 St. Louis Mary de Montfort, *True Devotion to Mary*, pg. 298.
13 St. Louis Mary de Montfort, *The Secret of the Rosary*, pp. 132-133.

LUMINOUS MYSTERIES

1 St. Louis Mary de Montfort, *True Devotion to Mary*, pg. 293.
2 Ibid.
3 The petitions in the Luminous Mysteries are written by the author in the style of St. Louis de Montfort.
4 St. Louis Mary de Montfort, *The Secret of the Rosary*, pp. 132-133.

PRAYER TO TRINITY

1 *Catechism of the Catholic Church.* 2nd ed. Vatican: Libreria Editrice Vaticana, 2000. Print. In-text citation: (Catholic Church 69).
2 Dom Augustine Marie, OSB, *The Message of Our Lady of Fatima (Selections)*, Google shortened URL: https://goo.gl/biem9Q, pg. 1. Accessed online February 23, 2017.

ABOUT THE AUTHOR

Meggie K. Daly is a Catholic revert. She retired from a fast-paced career in scientific research and technology development when her husband's job relocated them from a large city on the West Coast to a small community in the rural South.

She now teaches university mathematics part-time and writes as a member of the Catholic Writers Guild. Meggie is active in ministry in her home parish and teaches Adult Faith Formation classes as a professional catechist in her diocese. She is a consultant to several dozen Catholic parishes as part of a larger effort to help Catholics understand and love their faith.

An avid and determined gardener, Meggie is learning to make peace with high humidity and to share her roses and other flowers with Japanese beetles, squirrels, voles, and deer. She is married with six adult children and three grandchildren.

Made in United States
North Haven, CT
03 June 2023

37332185R00075